P9-DOII-223

Intuition @ Work

Intuition @ Work

& at Home and at Play

JAMES WANLESS

Red Wheel
Boston, MA / York Beach, ME

First published in 2002 by
Red Wheel/Weiser, LLC
York Beach, ME
With offices at:
368 Congress Street
Boston, MA 02210
www.redwheelweiser.com

Cataloging-in-Publication Data available upon request
from the Library of Congress.
ISBN 1-59003-012-5

Typeset in MetaPlusBook
Printed in the United States of America
Designed by Joyce C. Weston

MV
08 07 06 05 04 03 02
8 7 6 5 4 3 2 1
The paper used in this publication meets the minimum
requirements of the American National Standard for
Information Sciences—Permanence of Paper for Printed
Library Materials Z39.48-1992 (R1997).

CONTENTS

ACKNOWLEDGMENTS

I want to thank Rebecca Townsend for her promotion of my intuition work in Australia; the Kaiser Institute of Colorado for their support of intuition in the healthcare industry; my Merrill West Publishing business partner, Julie King, who knows what it's like to work with me; my partner and co-creator of our "expressive intelligence" program, Elisa Lodge, the genius; all my fellow Voyager Tarot travelers in consciousness; special people like Ron Tanner, Greg Brandenburgh, Marcel Zwart, Johannes Fiebig, Indira Aslan, Scott Bray; all the intuition coaches and authors, especially Nancy Rosanoff and Marcia Emery; the wildly creative energy of Garapata Beach, Big Sur; my 92-year-old dad and inspiration, Emery; and my most favorite of muses, Jolly, my cat, the "jollylama."

CONTENTS

ACKNOWLEDGMENTS

I want to thank Rebecca Townsend for her promotion of my intuition work in Australia; the Kaiser Institute of Colorado for their support of intuition in the healthcare industry; my Merrill West Publishing business partner, Julie King, who knows what it's like to work with me; my partner and co-creator of our "expressive intelligence" program, Elisa Lodge, the genius; all my fellow Voyager Tarot travelers in consciousness; special people like Ron Tanner, Greg Brandenburgh, Marcel Zwart, Johannes Fiebig, Indira Aslan, Scott Bray; all the intuition coaches and authors, especially Nancy Rosanoff and Marcia Emery; the wildly creative energy of Garapata Beach, Big Sur; my 92-year-old dad and inspiration, Emery; and my most favorite of muses, Jolly, my cat, the "jollylama."

INTUITION @ WORK

1

ULTIMATE RESOURCE

THE REWARDS OF INTUITION

> "One can never consent to creep when one feels an impulse to soar."
>
> —Helen Keller

All good things come from living intuitively. To follow that feeling inside of us we call our intuition is really the only way to fulfill our highest aspirations and deepest needs. Indeed, the intuitive impulse helps us soar.

We all want to find the path in life that will bring us happiness and love, abundance, good health, and meaning. Unlike our animal friends, who instinctively and unerringly know how to live to their fullest, we have many more choices to make, and thus much more doubt and confusion. How do we know our way? Nikos Kazantzakis, author of *Zorba the Greek*, once wrote, "As I watched the seagulls, I thought, 'That's the road to take; find the absolute rhythm and follow it with absolute trust.'" What is our absolute rhythm? The intuitive flow that naturally moves within us at all times.

Intuition is the life force itself, made conscious to us through a feeling that arises from within. Intuition is our human version of animal instinct. Through our intuition we tap the ultimate resource of all—the very source of life. By following the intuitive spirit all that each of us can humanly be and do is directly revealed and made manifest.

Intuition is an everyday way for everyone to connect with the divine. It is not necessary to be religious, meditate, pray, or be "psychic" to be intuitive. Our contact with the life spirit through intuition is ever-present and immediate. In fact, everyone is intuitive, naturally. Much of the time, however, we unconsciously follow it. And sometimes we don't—we let somebody else's belief, opinion, or dictate determine our life. The true intuitive person is consciously aware of the inner feeling and feels good about following the feeling. The intuitive life is the consciously felt life.

> "There is something within you that knows much more than you know."
> —Rochelle Myers, *Creativity in Business*

We can all probably recall an instance where our intuition guided us or saved us in some extraordinary or miraculous way. Reading *Newsweek* magazine recently, I ran across the story of Dana Colwell. As she recounts, "When I got up to put my clothes on one morning, I almost didn't wear a bra. But a higher power told me to put it on." Shortly, thereafter, she was hit in the chest with a nail, but was saved from serious injury by her liquid-padded bra.

My own intuition story goes back to my senior year

of high school. I was selected to participate in a series of competitive panels for achieving the distinction of being the top math and science student in the San Francisco Bay Area. I was hardly the best, but somehow I knew in advance what questions were going to be asked. My intuition was in action, and I won that award because I heeded that feeling inside of me.

Although I was mightily impressed by this mysterious power, I went on with my ordinary way of living. Many of us have encountered some great experience of precognition; yet I suspect we mostly view intuition as some uncontrollable, random phenomenon. Why don't we deliberately cultivate our intuitiveness? Is it because we believe it's only serendipitous? Is it because we aren't even aware that intuitions exist within us from moment to moment?

Because intuition emanates from the very mystery of life, it is often unrecognized and unobserved. It is even denigrated and dismissed as something so ineffable that it cannot be trusted.

I have written this book to explore how intuition is present in every moment of our lives and how it exists in many ways other than the occasional hunch. What this investigation has shown me is how much intuition can do for us and how easily it can be accessed. I believe our intuition is useful in a practical way, more so now than in any other time in human evolution, such that it has even become imperative for the survival of our species.

Opening the Big Mind

> "Genius, in truth, means little more than the
> faculty of perceiving in an unhabitual way."
> —Robert Olson, *The Art of
> Creative Thinking*

The key to unlocking the richness of our intuitive wisdom is to engage in extraordinary, perhaps even revolutionary, ways of comprehending our lives. Examples in this book of how to do this range from metaphoric and symbolic picture thinking, strategic storytelling, creative walking, art, and dreaming, to awareness meditation, "metasensory" smelling and tasting, consulting oracles, mind's-eye visualization, humming, fooling around, and most importantly, *feeling your feelings*.

The Authentic Life

Intuitions come from deep within us in such a way that they can bypass our socialization and our conditioned thoughts and beliefs. Intuitive feelings represent what is true for each of us as individual beings. Intuitive living is authentic living. True to ourselves, we can author and make the life that is absolutely right for us. Following our own inner authority, and no one else's, intuition tells us our needs and guides our desires. Then, all our decisions and actions come from the very essence of our own being. We can do no more than that.

> "You have got to discover you, what you do, and
> trust it."
>
> —Barbra Streisand

Only when we know ourselves and act ourselves, can we be truly, truly happy, for, as Jane Roberts writes in *The Nature of Personal Reality*, "You must trust yourself. If you do not, then you will forever be looking to others to prove your own merit to you, and you will never be satisfied."

Through intuition, we live out all that we can be and are meant to be. The seed of potential inherent within us at birth can grow uncompromised into fullness. There can be no greater joy and no greater purpose for living.

Genius

Intuition is the source of our own unique and natural genius. It's unfortunate that genius is equated with only mental intelligence. At the risk of sounding silly, everyone has genes, and thus genius. The genius of every living entity is in the particular way it expresses its own original being. True genius is found in authentic being, which encompasses how we express ourselves emotionally, physically, and mentally. The truer we are to ourselves, the more original we are. Nobody can be you as brilliantly as yourself—that is genius! This inimitable genius is our "genie," our own special power and magic. In truth, we are all magical. Within us are ingenious personal resources to make a richly fulfilling life.

Creativity

Intuition is the power of creation. The intuitive feeling within us contains the sum total and synergy of our whole being—at once, the aroused heart, the turned-on mind, and the activated body and spirit coming together. Inevitably and naturally, this turns into an alchemical union of creativity. Through intuition, we ourselves become the creative life source of constant innovation and invention and of renewal and regeneration. The meaningful and successful life is the one we intentionally create and recreate.

It seems as though we "try" to be creative, when all we have to do is follow the impulse that turns us on. Like genius, creativity is misunderstood; it is not about skills, but about courage, the courage to trust inspiration and keep going with it until we break through the conventional norms. If we have the will, as Tom Robbins writes in *Silver Departures,* "we push it into the wildest edge of edges; then you force it into the realm of magic." Intuition is wild and free, and when we ride on its back, we tap into the bloodstream of the universe, the etheric juice of all creation.

Energy

Intuition is energy! Intuitions are impulses that move us. Nothing is ever done without energy, and the more energy we have, the greater the life we lead. Energy is not a sexy word, but the bottom line explanation for success in any life endeavor is the energy we have. With enough energy, anything is possible. We can make mistakes and we can dawdle along, but as long as we have energy, we get along just fine.

It's funny that we look for all sorts of energy techniques, drinks, and tablets to give us energy when, if we would just pay attention to the feelings that have a charge for us, we would find that it's flowing through us all the time. The intuitive spark, by virtue of being the life force itself, gives us natural, easy, swift, and seemingly effortless and enduring energy. It keeps going and going and going.

As much as there are sometimes energy crises in the world, there can be energy crises within us. We are working harder, doing more, sleeping less, and becoming more fatigued. But if we move with the intuitive flow, we can maintain and sustain, on and on.

Productivity and Results

Intuitive living is active living. The energy of the intuitive impulse ignites us into action. In this physical world of ours, we are meant to be physical. Nothing gets done without doing. When we don't heed our inner voice, we procrastinate, live in our thoughts, and achieve neither our visions and dreams nor our destiny. Following our intuition, we proact, perform, and produce. Intuitions get things started and completed.

The process of acting catalyzes intuitive creativity and genius. If you don't know what to do or how to do, just start doing, and everything will become clear. This may sound a bit heretical, but I have found in my counseling work that if I don't know what to say, I just start talking. The physical act of speech itself ultimately triggers what I want to communicate. Let the body lead; its cells contain eons of wisdom and intuitive creativity. So, if you don't know where to go, just start walking. If you don't know what to write, just start writing.

Good Decisions

We are all faced with decisions, decisions, decisions. In this world of change, complexity, uncertainty, multiplicity, and speed, good decision-making has become difficult and vexing. Fortunately for us, intuition directs our actions so that we are decisive and correct.

How does this work? Intuition is the great synthesizer of all that we know. It carries the sum total of what our mind thinks and imagines, how our heart feels, and what our body senses. It even recalls the experiences from our subconscious memories. It is the fullest use of all our intelligences. If we consciously follow it, our course of action is right for us, because our whole being is in agreement.

We always want to be right, right? The truth is that there are very few instances of objective right-doing. Right decisions are subjective, true for us and maybe for no one else. Good decisions are those that we totally stand behind. In our whole truth, we are in our integrity and power. We are at our greatest capacity to effect the results we desire. What more can we do?

Gift of Prescience

Good decisions always take into account our picture of what we see happening as a result of our actions. Our mind's eye is a very powerful intuitive tool for visioning the future. So-called "psychics" are those with an active imagination. The reality is that we are all psychic if we would just be attentive to the pictures that cross our mind when considering anything. The pictures are always there—but are we conscious of them?

The ability to forecast means slowing down and remembering to look at the images our forebrain casts on the screen of our inner eye of imagination. This is not easy in our world, where we are constantly bombarded with pictures from outside of us through television, films, magazines, and computer screens. Our so-called "third eye" gets lazy as we depend upon external picturing for stimuli, as we read fewer books, and as we are inundated with useless information. It's time to be our own "tell-a-vision," our own dream machine, our own information network. In not doing so, we sabotage our own power and abnegate our future to the networks, the agencies, the studios, the publishers—to everyone but ourselves.

Healthy and Fit

It might seem odd that in talking about intuition the issue of health arises. Intuitive awareness, by its very nature, is all-comprehensive and takes in how the body is responding from moment to moment. Intuitions are always expressed in the body and are always good for the body. The more we tune into them, the deeper and keener is our sensitivity to what's going on physiologically. Unaware of our intuition, we are unaware of our bodies. Not following our intuition, the body suffers. It's just natural that in adhering to our intuition, we do right by our body. It's as simple as that.

The intuitive body is not about muscles, firmness, or good looks but is flexible, in motion and in balance, a body that dances. The open, pliable, loose intuitive body seems more naturally feminine, but women have a tendency to dislike their bodies for one cosmetic reason or another. Men seek a strong, hard body that is anti-intuitive in its rigidity and density. Intuition flows like water, so intuitive bodies are fluid and flowing. For men, even our dress—pants, belts, and ties—is confining and tight—more like industrial-age uniforms than intuitive-age freedom wear.

The intuitive body is sensual. The more intuitively attuned we become, the more sensitive we are. We regain our senses—we truly taste, touch, smell, hear, and see, rather than just enclose ourselves in our think-ing minds. Sensitizing our bodies by intuitive acuity, we reclaim the genuine attractiveness of a sensual, flow-ing, and feeling body that emanates an aura of authen-ticity, alertness, and energy.

The Healing Power of Love

Intuition is our own healer, our friend for life, and ally in our most difficult times. If we listen to it closely, it will tell us how to rebalance our lives. For me and my own pathology of "chronic fatigue," intuition tells me when to slow down, stop, and rest; what to eat; and how to reach out and be kind to myself. It's when I am pushing and working hard, trying to do things that I think, in my socially conditioned mind, are necessary, that I go down. All in all, I am neither listening to myself nor being myself at the deepest of levels. I am not caring for myself, not being true to myself, not loving myself. I have found that intuition is like a lover, an uncondi-tional and compassionate embrace from within of loving wisdom that exists only to serve ourselves in always the most positive of ways. It will never deny us and is always with us. Hold it dearly.

> "The inner voice—the human compulsion when deeply distressed to seek healing counsel within ourselves both to create this counsel and to receive it."
>
> —Alice Walker, *You Can't Keep a Good Woman Down*

Remember the phrase, "a little birdie told me." That's what intuition is, like a little birdie, or perhaps an angel or a genie. When we get in trouble, it's because we have not been true to our own angel, our own eternal lover. There is always a way through the difficult times; just listen to the deepest, most authentic voice and feeling of *you*. Know there will be the distractions of thoughts and ideas coming from different people that we have internalized. They are not you, nor are they your way. The true and only course of life and love is present now and always.

Expanded Consciousness

Intuitiveness demands keen awareness—awareness of the deepest part of ourselves; of our past, present, and future; of our body and mind; of our visions and dreams; and of sensory and extrasensory information. True intuitiveness requires cognizance of the distorted lens through which we may view the world, for we can deny authentic intuition by emotional reactions that are projections of unfounded insecurities and fears.

The intuitive person is always probing and exploring what is accurately going on inside, while aware and responsive to what is happening outside. Intuitive living is awake and alert. Fully conscious, we are quite simply more on top of things. We are smarter, quicker, wiser, healthier. Our real ongoing education is not in the university but in the universe of the self — not *higher* learning but *deeper* learning.

This is why learning a meditation practice is invaluable. The essence of meditation, regardless of its particular type, is "mindfulness"—nonjudgmental awareness of what we are sensing, thinking, and feeling from moment to moment. A formal training in sitting meditation gives us the grounding to practice the most important kind of meditation, being mindful at all times throughout our day.

True Communication and Real Relationships

The fully conscious, intuitive person is aware of the surrounding world—events, trends, and, most importantly, others. In our populous and interactive world of constant communication with people, the richness of our lives may be measured by the quality of our relationships. Whether it's talking to a friend, parenting a child, meeting a work associate, leading a group, making a sale, writing an e-mail, or being with a lover, intuitive empathy is the bond that solidifies and deepens the connection. People-to-people intuition is the empathic ability to feel what another feels. We are all born with the gift of "reading" people—of hearing below their words, of seeing through their mask, of sensing the truth, of feeling another's joy or pain.

This intuitive understanding leads to a kind of communication that creates true community, for there becomes, ultimately, nothing to hide. And feeling what others feel, we identify with them and know that we are all in the same boat. Honesty results, which is the bottom line for success in all relationships. Trying to posture, defend, use, or gain advantage are useless and ineffective. Instead of power over people and the distrust it engenders, we experience the real relationship of human to human. Ahh, how good does that feel?

Women of Power

I confess that I feel, sense, believe, and know that women are more intuitively attuned than men, if for no other reason than that they are more likely to be introspective. In my work as a facilitator of self-discovery and empowerment, women predominate. I am sure there are other reasons for women's intuitiveness, but the plain truth for me is that I see women as more in touch with their emotions, their bodies, their psychologies. And I experience women as more in touch with others. They relate to relate.

Many women know, but they keep silent. They allow their men to carry on and be in charge. I feel that if women were absolutely honest with themselves and were to *act* on their intuition, they would come into power in our political and economic institutions. And perhaps the world would be a more compassionate and cooperative one.

> "The here, the now, and the individual, have always been the special concern of the saint, the artist, the poet—and from time immemorial—the woman. In the small circle of home, she has never quite forgotten the particular uniqueness of each member of the family; the spontaneity of now; the vividness of here. This is the basic substance of life. These are the individual elements that form the bigger entities like mass, future, world."
>
> —Anne Morrow Lindbergh, *Gift from the Sea*

Men of Whole Life

> "By opening up to the inflow of the Divine Feminine on an intuitive level, each person can experience a profound blessing that can affect how we relate to each moment of our daily life. Our world becomes more alive, vibrant, and interesting."
>
> —Robert Powell, *The Sophia Teachings*

We men are intuitive, but we do not pay as much attention to our intuition, nor do we value it. Intuition is often dismissed as a "women's thing," when really it is a "divine" thing. We are caught by thought. We tend to be conceivers rather than feelers. We are more achievers than relaters. None of this has to be true, however.

If men were to acknowledge and respect their intuitions, what would they gain? A more complete way of living, because intuition encompasses the whole being. Some men may become obsessed by worldly achievement and think that is what they must do to define and prove themselves, but their intuition may be saying, "Hey, take it easy, look after your health, and do what you really love and value." The wholeness of intuition leads to a life where feelings and fortunes, people and products, inner self and outer world, and the receptive and assertive are equally treasured. It would be a life that men would live more fully and wholly, that would be more about quality than quantity, more about process than payoffs. It would be a life about spirituality as much as materiality and about long-range posterity as well as short-term gain. It would balance stillness and speed, reflection and action. Richness would be defined by this balance and by healthiness and depth of being. Men would be happier, and thus the world would be a happier place.

The Intuitive Man

In rereading the paragraph above, I see it as a classic male and "*men*-tal" way of "describing" things, or rather, "listing" them, as men tend to do. This study of intuition has made me more aware of the nature and depth of women's intuition and has triggered a shift in my own way of perception. Men need to consciously practice intuition. I have even practiced feeling my own inner feminine energy as a way of developing my intuition. I can honestly say that when I do, I see life from a more whole way of being, a kind of whole-brain way of thinking that is more intuitive. In fact, the scientific evidence, according to CAT scans, is that when women consider something, their whole brain lights up, whereas for men, it is only a narrowly focused area.

The question is, how as a man can I be more whole-brained? The chance that I will grow my corpus callosum in this lifetime is probably slim. This is the connecting tissue between the right and left hemispheres of the brain, which is larger in women than in men and is conducive to whole-brain activity. So, what I do is soften the body and soften the eyes and allow in the feelings of whatever I am considering. I see and think with the whole body. It's difficult to describe, but perception does change. It is more comprehensive, allowing in a greater variety of mental, emotional, and sensory information simultaneously.

A second intuitive practice for men is not to compartmentalize so much. I am sure women have wondered at our male ability to turn on and off so suddenly. So, I have been deliberately writing this book on my raspberry-colored iMac on the counter between my kitchen and living room so as to incorporate a regular kind of busy house and life situation into my work and my intuitive awareness. At first it was difficult, and I was not too happy, but I kept at it, and now I truly like it. In me was a vague and distant inner voice and knowing (intuition) that it was the right thing to do. Now my mind is more relaxed as I write, it's more open and more natural. The spigot of intuitive creativity has been turned on.

A couple of the quotes from women in this book have also had a profound impact on me and my intuitive development. One, by Jenny Read, is that the world needs less light and more warmth. Wow, warmth! That felt so good and so true to me (intuition) upon reading it that I've been "warming up" my writing ever since by a more personal tone. We men try so hard to be smart and to enlighten the world that we get abstract, idea-oriented, and arid cold in our thinking and living. Intuition is about human being and feeling our way through life. In bringing more real-life situations and emotions into the mix, we not only warm up others so they can better understand us, but we warm up our own intuitive, feeling sensitivities.

To be warmer, I have included more writing from a personal perspective. In truth, much of my research into intuition has been by self-observation and experience. Intuition is personal, after all. Another potent quote was by Marya Mannes, who states that women cannot help but take things personally. Men tend to depersonalize, which is opposite to the intuitive way. My advice to men is to look at issues and subjects from a personally experienced viewpoint. Then the intuitive truth will emerge.

Needless to say, I was genuinely surprised to learn that the leadership manual for the U.S. Military Academy emphasizes, "Be, know, do." "Being" comes first, and West Pointers are some of our greatest leaders in the business world and in society generally. What is meant by *being*? Understanding yourself—what you stand for, your purpose, your self-concept, your own code of ethics, *who you are*. This inner core of being is lasting and the place of real power.

Is it possible that what we would ordinarily consider a bastion of lockstep living and straitjacket thinking, the military academy, has flip-flopped into a more intuition-oriented way of thinking and leading? Yes, and the reason why is that the world has changed so dramatically that for the cadets to survive—not only in war but in life—they've had to become more flexible. Mark Hoffman, a former West Pointer who is now Chairman and CEO of Commerce One says, "When you go into battle, order quickly disintegrates, and you have to take action with limited information." That's where intuition comes in, and that's where knowing and trusting yourself is critical.

Healing the Imbalance of the Sexes

The intuitive way of life is revolutionary for our world. One revolutionary effect is a greater equality of the genders. I view the inequality between men and women in today's world as the single greatest dysfunction of humankind. As long as the old patriarchal power system prevails, society will be out of balance and diseased. Such an imbalance is not the natural way of life. Unless balance is achieved, our species and our world are at risk.

Women achieving positions of economic/political power and men opening to the whole life will heal the divide. Women don't have to be only from Venus and men only from Mars. In the merger, a creative synergy takes place that evolves the world to a more sustainable consciousness for humankind and the planet.

Success in Navigating the Business of Living

My own conscious entry into the intuitive inner worlds was through meditation and spiritual seeking, but during the course of making a living, it has become clear to me that a business approach to life sharpens the use of our intuitive skills. Certainly this is true in formal business. Businesspeople must look into the future, be innovative, make difficult decisions in uncertain conditions, be adroit at handling relationships and clients, and keep moving with action and energy under the pressure of performance—all of these being qualities in which intuition excels.

Many of the examples and quotes that I use are from the business world because business is at the forefront of exploring applied intuition. This is particularly so now in light of our complex, changing, and fast-paced business world.

The truth is, however, that whoever we are and whatever we do, we are all in business. As in the business world, we all produce and exchange our services and goods. Even a child is in business, producing a smile or a finger painting in exchange for the security provided by the parent. A housewife and mother produces and serves all day long so that her children and husband benefit, and in return she is rewarded with their love, sense of family, and security.

In fact, all the techniques and quotes from businesspeople, executives, and famous people in this book are absolutely valid for all aspects of our own lives. Perhaps, you want to be more creative in the home or with your family. The ideas expressed by great scientists and artists in the chapter on creativity apply, as do the insights of CEOs in the communication and decision-making chapters.

Actually, the business approach to life gives our existence greater meaning. Whether it's the business of a relationship, a family, or a corporation, we are here on earth to create and share who we are and what we have to offer as our service. Out of that, community is created, and we all profit, whether it's by increased love, friendship, money, or wisdom. With this greater purpose and intention in our interactions, rather than just "getting along," we navigate our life course more consciously and responsibly, which inevitably means more intuitively.

The business of a life of creating, interacting, exchanging, and receiving forces us to know ourselves, who we are, what we produce, our own value, what we value in trade, and how to get that.

> **"If I didn't define myself for myself, I would be crunched into other people's fantasies for me and eaten alive."**
> —Audre Lorde

The business of living is, fundamentally, a set of relationships; so we must understand others and even the relationship itself. All these interpersonal dynamics require intuitive "reads" and assessments, intuitively directed inspirations, strategies, and decisions.

The business of living is an active one. It requires taking action on our intuitive feelings. And the best way to develop intuition is to act on it! In keeping with intuition's uncomplicated and essentially preverbal quality, I have written this handbook as an action manual. It shows you how to use it, apply it, practice it, exercise it, and explore it in your everyday world at any time in this business called life.

Intuition Application: Remember to Feel

Ask and ask again, "How am I feeling?" So, how do you feel, actually, at this very moment as you read this? And as you read this book, continue to ask, "How am I feeling?"

2 THE INTUITIVE IMPERATIVE

INTELLIGENCE FOR THE TWENTY-FIRST CENTURY

> "As human beings, our greatness lies not so much in being able to remake the world. . . as in being able to remake ourselves."
> —Mahatma Gandhi

In the speeding, changing, revolutionary world of the twenty-first century, it is more difficult than ever to steer a clear course in the business of living. We can communicate faster from New York to London via fiber optics than from our brain to the tip of our fingers. How do we keep up? It is estimated that we have 170 interactions with others every business day. How do we maintain all of our diverse communications and partnerships in this growing relationship world? We all know that life has become dauntingly complex and uncertain. How do we know anything for sure anymore? At the dawning of our extraordinary evolution in human quality of life brought about through the great advances of the sciences and technology, we are challenged by the fact that our own internal human way of managing life is under threat.

While we have achieved unparalleled prosperity, we

are working harder and multi-tasking more than ever before. We are expected to be continuously creating and changing, even as change itself is changing. The result is stress, anxiety, fatigue, burnout, addiction, and disease. In short, the human being is under assault— our physical, emotional, and mental resources are becoming strained to capacity.

A new human technology must emerge if we are to thrive with the promise of the life we all desire. To match the outside social, economic, and technological forces of change, solutions must come from within us, within our own human being. By deliberately tapping our intuition—that knowing feeling—a heretofore undervalued and underused innate human genius, we have a natural technology for energizing and navigating our lives. Through intuition, we have a tool for becoming more intelligent and conscious, and on a practical down-to-earth side, more efficient and effective.

> "Intuition is the new physics. It's an Einsteinian, seven-sense, practical way to make tough decisions. The crazier the times are, the more important it is for leaders to develop and trust their intuition."
> —Tom Peters, in *Fast Company,* March 2001

Intuition is, fortunately, a skill that everyone has. It is free and accessible to all. Intuition is simple. Intuition is quick. In fact, what has stayed its development is its inherent ease. It's so ordinary, we ask, how can it have power and value?

Like a muscle, though, intuition can be greatly developed through exercise. We are just now beginning to recognize its potential. We are at a very early stage of intuition's maturation into an accepted way of cognitive knowing, personal guidance, professional management, and everyday living.

Only recently, in 1997, did a monumental, groundbreaking study by neuroscientists at the University of Iowa Medical College show that intuition is, in fact, an empirical skill hardwired into our physical brain. Located in the emotional part of the prefrontal lobe in the forebrain, intuitions arise as a kind of subconscious "feeling." Once the participants in the study began to trust the feeling, they never erred in their judgment during the battery of tests they underwent.[1]

A guiding principle in the evolution of life is that the qualities of an environment that place a species at risk are the very conditions that can stimulate new adaptive powers and growth. Fortunately, intuition thrives on those very circumstances of our modern business of living that challenge us. Moreover, intuition keeps up with the speed of our technological life, for it is so fast that it seems instantaneous. A feeling comes before we picture or think about anything. And intuition feeds on change, as it is inherently and always responsive to the present moment. Akin to instinct, intuition is a survival skill that comes to the fore out of struggles like the competitive demands of our new economy. Intuition has no problem with the complex information load we all bear, for it is a natural integrator—synthesizing and simplifying all that we have heard, read, seen, experienced, and subconsciously absorbed. And it flourishes in states of ambiguity, for it is a mysterious faculty and power designed for uncertainty.

By transforming the demons of our twenty-first-century life into opportunities for our intuitive development, we can relish and utilize these "problems" as resources. We, and not outside forces, will be in better command of our lives again. It is clear to me that those who seize this opportunity will be our leaders.

As I intuitively peer into the future, one thing I see for sure is that there is going to be. . . MORE! More of everything. More than ever before, each of us will be required to make more independent choices among mounting alternatives in all aspects of life, and intuition is our clearest decision-making tool. In addition, with more change, we will have to be more innovative in making up our lives, and intuition is naturally a creative force. With change happening more rapidly, we must look ahead more to plan for the future, and intuition is the unique gift and genius of human foresight. Because the world is becoming increasingly populous and networked, we will need better communication skills, and intuition is the basis for all effective communication, whether it be in partnering, teaming, befriending, or leading. Due to the increasing demands of our growing world, we will require more personal energy, and intuition, as we shall see, conserves and creates energy by its very nature.

Obsolescent Thinking

> "Man, surrounded by facts, permitting himself no surprise, no intuitive flash, no great hypothesis, no risk, is in a locked cell. Ignorance cannot seal the mind and imagination more securely."
> —Lillian Smith, *The Journey*

Thinking intelligence in this world today is often too slow, too limiting, and too linear for the dynamic, diverse, and ambiguous nature of the times. Just twenty years ago, a group of leading thinkers met at MIT to discuss the future of the personal computer and concluded that it would only be useful to shut-ins and otherwise handicapped persons. How many thinkers ten years ago predicted the most dominant development of today, the Internet? And what thinkers thought that the Internet-driven new economy would collapse so suddenly and severely? Overdependence on your analytic intellect will render you obsolete.

> "A great many people think they are thinking, when they are merely rearranging their prejudices."
> —William James

In a telling and insightful comment by Steve Ballmer, CEO of Microsoft, he stated that his greatest downfall as an executive was in being too logical and linear in his thinking, thus not taking the quantum leap of vision that would have propelled his company quickly into the forefront of e-commerce.

> "Reason presents itself as the solution to the problems it has created."
> —John Ralston Saul

Intuition Application: Intuitive Sensing

What feels hot to you about the future in your business, and what feels cold? What deal smells good, and what smells bad? What situation tastes sweet, and what tastes fishy? What opportunity sounds good, and what sounds off? What option feels heavy, and what feels light?

Big Mind to the Rescue

Intuition is what I call the "big mind." In the dictionary, intuition is generally defined as what we "know before thinking." This cognitive ability is inclusive, integrating *all* the ways in which we know and understand, through a "feeling."

This intuitive feeling draws up all the information stored in our subconscious memory bank of experience. It includes all of our emotions, which research now shows have real and measurable intelligence. It incorporates what our physical body senses, as well as our extrasensory perception, which picks up on ideas and feelings that exist as vibratory energies in the airwaves of the invisible electromagnetic world. Intuition even taps into the so-called collective unconscious, the ultimate data bank of human history and evolution.

Intuition also includes what is true for our thinking mind, whether by logical or lateral forms of thinking. Not an enemy of thought, intuition wants as many ideas put into the mix of our conscious awareness as possible. So, thinking smart and getting the basics of traditional education is imperative.

> "The purpose of thinking is to so arrange the world (in our minds) that we can apply emotion effectively. In the end, it is emotion that makes the choices and decisions."
> —Edward De Bono, *Teach Your Child How to Think*

Call for a New Intelligence

As we know, traditional values and ways of succeeding are being turned inside out. In the past, we thought that literacy and reasoning skills were the way to succeed in life, and so we've been educated in the so-called 3Rs of reading, writing and arithmetic. I can remember spending my entire seventh grade year memorizing the multiplication tables. For what? I now ask. In our topsy-turvy world, these fundamental abilities, while necessary, are not primary values. In fact, study after study has shown that what is demanded in the twenty-first-century world and economy are inner qualities such as self-initiative, interpersonal empathy, and "emotional intelligence."[2]

Intuition is the core skill for all these new qualities. Consider taking *initiative*. In this twenty-first-century world, we are all becoming leaders of our personal and business lives. The initiative required of leadership is the strength of what we personally *feel* as the best course of action. The only way to be an initiator in life is to be mentored and moved by our own feelings.

Intuition actually means, "in-tuition," or learning and being educated from inside ourselves. Only when we are following the wisdom of our inner feelings, which may be expressed in a vision, thought, voice, or hunch, are we authentic. Then we are a genuinely self-led person.

Once we contact the feeling within, our *emotional intelligence* (EQ) determines how to respond so that it's appropriate and not extreme to the point of dysfunctional behavior. The connection between a subconscious feeling arising from the mystery of life and an emotionally intelligent action is our intuition, which is discerned through our ability to be consciously aware of what we are feeling, without judgment. This so-called "fair witnessing" of the feeling is similar to a meditative-like awareness of feeling without attachment. This pure kind of awareness of the feeling inevitably gives us a feeling about the feeling, which leads us to the appropriate response. True intuitive intelligence incorporates acute sensitivity to inner feelings with emotionally intelligent response. As Robert Cooper and Ayman Sawaf write in *Executive EQ:*

> Intuition is one of the most sought-after qualities in an entrepreneur or leader. It is closely related to, and can transcend, emotional intelligence. It *moves* us and, at an advanced level, we learn to enter intuitive flow by choice rather than chance . . . Intuition is a heightened dimension of emotional intelligence.

Interpersonal empathy—the heart of healthy communication by the ability to read others' feelings and be skilled in handling the emotional dynamics of relationships—is, again, an intuitive gift. Through our intuition we have a feeling sense of what is going on with another and how best to interact with them.

Revolutionary Wisdom for Revolutionary Times

"The purpose of today's training is to defeat yesterday's understanding."
—Miyamoto Musashi,
sixteenth-century swordsman

It often has been said that we cannot solve anything by the same method it was created. We need revolutionary approaches to our revolutionary world. Going within ourselves to purely and clearly feel the feeling is revolutionary, creating as much a revolution in our personal lives as in the world we are witnessing around us. Though it's easy once you get it, it's not initially easy to consciously identify and follow true feelings, for all our learning and socialization go against it. We are taught to either follow along, or to reason things out. Emphasis on the accepted habitual way and on our mental intelligence detracts from our awareness of what we are feeling from moment to moment.

The truth is that our human genius comes through our feelings first, and then into our thoughts. Uncensored feelings cannot be programmed or predicted. Spontaneous, unreasoned, and mysterious, they come directly from the life force. Feelings are original and originating. As messengers from the life source, they inherently carry ingenious wisdom.

FEEL THE FEELING

THE INTUITION PORTAL

> "Neurosis consists in being out of touch with
> one's own feelings and sensory experiences,
> and therapy is the recovery of awareness."
> —Fritz Perls

Knowing from within—through feeling our feelings—is the essence of intuitiveness. Though this is an inherent human gift, many of us do not often consciously feel our feelings. Even when we do, we sometimes resist and reject them. Emotional insensitivity and repression block intuition and lead to counterintuitive behavior.

How can we get back in touch with our feelings? By going to the source of their repression, which is our fear that acting out our true feelings brings disapproval. Emotions are irrational, outside of reason, often running counter to how we are supposed to act. They can upset the conventional norms of behavior. So when we feel in a way that is out of synch with how we are taught to feel and be, this can lead to being criticized, ostracized, and rejected, which is what many of us experience early on in our childhood. We learn to shut up, bury the feeling, and follow along. It's easier to be

conditionally loved than honest. Most modern psycho-
therapy strives to expose this fear of being unloved and
unaccepted, and encourages the release of whatever
we are feeling.

> "Mary Kay Ash had a gut feeling that women who
> could acknowledge their self-worth would indeed
> become very successful marketers and entrepre-
> neurs."
> —Pelton, et al., *Tough Choices: Decision-Making
> Styles of America's Top 50 CEOs*

Intuitiveness is about having the courage to be authentic. It requires absolute trust and belief in ourselves.
Self-value and self-esteem are imperative to intuitive
being. Building self-worth seems like a lifetime's worth
of working to replace early social conditioning. Certainly books, support groups, friends, self-affirmations,
therapy—anything and anyone that unconditionally
accepts and encourages who we are can be helpful and
necessary to our healing. Restoring our personal
integrity is a healing process of becoming whole, of
closing the wounding that separates us from ourselves.

> "Having self-esteem is about more than repeating
> certain mantras to yourself each morning. . . .
> Even more, it's about trusting what your own
> heart is telling you."
> —Oprah Winfrey

Intuitive living requires a supportive environment for it
to thrive. One of the most essential is the environment

of our language. The words we use constitute a primary set of conditions that define how we see and live in the world. We are accustomed to saying, "I *think* that. . ." Try to say, "I *feel* that. . ." You will find it makes a major difference, bringing you back to your intuition.

Because we have neglected our emotions, we have lost an emotional vocabulary. Generally, when asked how we feel, we say, "OK" or "fine." These catchall words are meaningless, a cop-out. When we try to further define the actual state of our feelings, we are at a loss. Write down a list of words that more accurately and precisely describe your emotions, and begin to use them. Instead of feeling OK, in fact, we are probably feeling happy, or angry, or afraid, or sad, or peaceful, or loving. Words are eggs; they bring to life what is within us, so handle them with delicate awareness and intention.

The absolute key to restoring conscious intuition is *remembering* to consult your feelings. The single most important thing you can do to be intuitive is to be aware of how you are feeling from moment to moment.

Intuition Application: What to Wear

Probably your first intuitive act during the day is deciding what clothes to wear, which is a feeling based upon your mood and your intuitive read of the upcoming events of the day. Let that be a ritual for remembering to be intuitive during your day. Ask your intuition why you wore the color and outfit you have on today.

Intuition Application: Experiment and Practice

Try to intuit beforehand certain things in your daily life. This has much greater value than just a "guessing game." It truly does develop your intuitiveness. I have a friend who intuits which elevator will reach her first. I intuit how many e-mails I will have in the morning or if there is a cop on the road or where the fog on the coast is not going to be. Keep experimenting and playing. Even create an intuition practice like mine, trying to comprehend through the whole body in a warmer more personal way. This will keep your intuition faculty active. Use it or lose it.

We remember to feel our feelings if we are so motivated. By looking at how we actually make decisions in life, we clearly see how they are almost always unconsciously intuitive. Then we are inspired to pay attention to them. The more we are aware of and believe in intuition, the more effectively it works, for then it is not distorted by the impediment of habitual, linear, and critical ways of analytical thinking.

Intuition Application: Review Your Decisions

To become more consciously intuitive, ask yourself what decisions you made today that were not ultimately based upon a feeling? When do you make decisions that are absolutely rational, based upon adding up every conceivable pro and con that is measurable and that everyone would agree upon?

> **"We don't see things as they are, we see them as we are."**
> **—Anais Nin**

The All-Important Inner Work

Once we begin to feel our feelings, consciously and continuously, we run into another potential block that must be overcome. Because we have repressed our feelings, we tend to take on styles of behavior or character roles that help us get the approval and love we desire. These are like masks; they hide our true emotions, and so we don't feel the actual full range of feelings, which is what intuition demands. We become emotionally unbalanced, and hence, our intuition is often skewed and off. Cognizing through the perceptual lens of "how we are," we are feeling, acting, and being only in set habitual ways and seeing reality through a constricted and distorted lens. We are not being fully authentic, fully human—fully intuitive.

There are seven of these basic personality styles; let's examine them. Some people choose the role of "harmonizer." Like a chameleon, they go along with the prevailing emotion of others in order to get along. They bias their feelings toward seeing things as peaceful, or not peaceful. Others take on the persona of the "critic," putting down an idea or another person to build themselves up through the expression of intellectual arrogance. These types tend toward feeling negative anger, and they project that into their intuitions. Another role type is the optimistic "Pollyanna," only wanting to see things in the best light. They are prone to only feelings of happiness and joy—or not. There are "shy," or hermit, types who want to avoid and escape notice because of their insecurity. These kinds of people feel more fear than is warranted. The "martyr" types make sacrifices and get approval through sympathy. Their predominant feelings come through as sorrow and blame. The "overachiever" types act out in their way because they are tilted toward intuitive feelings of guilt. The "rationalizers" use their predominant feelings of shame to always be right.

These habitual personality styles are essentially defenses, ways of emotionally protecting ourselves and thus closing ourselves off from feeling all of our true feelings. But every kind of emotion is a valid intuitive message, and in our defensiveness and thus limited range of feeling, we cannot accurately read a situation or a person or a decision. There will be distortion, delusion, and denial.

> **"The truth will set you free. But first, it will piss you off."**
> —Gloria Steinem

It is critical to our intuitive development that we do the "inner work" of self-reflection that will lead to modification of our internal responses and outward behavior. The book *Emotional Alchemy* by Tara Bennett-Goleman is an excellent instructional text on clearing our dysfunctional emotional patterns.

Again, one of the crucial aspects of our personal growth is reaching a state of self-love and self-respect (we cannot expect those around us to give us approval). Secure with ourselves, we can let go of our defensiveness and its compensating excessive role egoism. The healthier we are emotionally, the more balanced we are in our ability to feel the complete range of possible truths. Our menu of choices and options is greatly enlarged, as is our ability to pursue them. In revolutionary times like ours, full of flux and ambiguity, balanced, open persons are best able to manage and lead an effective life.

Intuition Application: Your Personality Type

Determine your dominant personality type. How do you habitually tend to feel and, because of these feelings, interpret the world around you? Which feelings do you rarely get? Why is that?

The big mind of intuition and the revolutionary nature of our new world require letting go of our old world of "egonomics" in which we hold on to tightly constructed self-images and defensive behaviors that artificially protect and puff ourselves up. The best thing you can do to improve your intuitiveness, other than remembering to consult it again and again, is to take some courses in personal development to process out emotional insecurities and fear-based ways of perceiving reality.

This may eventually take you beyond a psychological way of self-balancing and into a greater metaconsciousness that opens up to the spiritual dimension of our being. A spiritual perspective enables us to trust the essential mystery of our intuitions. Spirituality helps us embrace all of life and all aspects of ourselves as one—a requisite for developed and heightened intuitiveness because conscious intuition is holistic and comprehensive.

4 INTUITIVE DECISION-MAKING

CHOOSING WISELY

> **"The most important quality of leadership is decisiveness."**
>
> **—Lee Iacocca**

Decision-making has never been as important and yet as difficult as it is today. In our world today, everyone has become a decision maker, and because of change, uncertainty, complexity, and volume of information and possibilities, decisions are not easy.

How do you make a decision when you do not know what will happen as a result? Trust your gut feeling. There is no other way. This is why a study by the American Institute of Management showed that the greater the decision-making responsibility of a business executive, the more intuitiveness was displayed.[3] Studies at Harvard Business School found that small business owners attribute 80 percent of their success to acting on intuition.[4] There is a direct correlation between responsibility and intuitive response-ability.

> **"Executives use intuition during *all* phases of the problem-solving process."**
>
> **—Daniel Isenberg, in**
> ***Harvard Business Review,* Dec. 1984**

One of the ultimate intuitive environments today is Internet e-business where high-speed deal making is commonplace. Here is what some of the most successful e-commerce entrepreneurs have to say. Tom Guilfoile, controller of Lycos, a leading Net portal company: "We rely a lot more on instinct than on facts. . . you have to become a good 'reader' of a company's people and its culture." Steve Jurvetson, of Draper Fisher Jurvetson, which has financed blockbuster Web companies says, "We don't do a lot of deep thinking, we never use Excel spreadsheets, we don't build models, we get a 'sense' of what will be an opportunity." Kevin O'Connor of the Web advertising superpower, Double-Click, says, "There is a certain amount of intuition in every Internet deal. You're operating on faith. You're trading speed for information." [5]

Do You Trust?

> "Intuition is what you know for sure without knowing for certain."
> —Weston Agor, *Intuition in Organizations*

Intuitive decision-making means having trust in yourself, in spite of being uncertain. Great decision-makers and leaders always have a high sense of self-esteem. Self-doubt destroys decisiveness. Even if you are not sure of yourself, you must "act as if" you are, even if that means simply having faith, a blind belief in your innate ability. It has been said that, "You cannot know the depth of the ocean until you have lost sight of the shore." We will never know our personal depth nor direct our life to its fullest and most authentic expression unless we let go of our desire to "know for sure" before making a decision.

> **"Toto, I've a feeling we're not in Kansas anymore."**
> **—Dorothy, in *The Wizard of Oz***

I can vividly recall the feeling I had upon completion of my doctorate work at Columbia University. I felt I had to leave academia; indeed I was not in "Kansas" anymore, but where was I? What was I to do? Go where? The only thing I knew for sure was that I had to go. As a friend of mine once said, "Do what you know." The rest, who knows? Trusting the feeling, I left the country; I just went. That act of pure trust and nothing else led me on to an unpredictable and wondrous life—my own Oz.

Intuition Application: Do You Trust Your Intuition?

Review in your life those hunches that have led to success. Take a look at the times you did not trust your intuition and what happened as a result.

> **"She was dimly aware of something within herself, competent, self-directive; she meant to trust it."**
> **—Mary Austin, *Earth Horizon***

Do You Believe?

Intuition takes the belief that the answer is within you. Following authorities, influences, and voices outside of yourself is unintuitive. Anita Roddick, founder of The Body Shop, is a believer in her own intuition, which usually runs counter to industry trends. She says, "I watch where the cosmetics industry is going and then walk in the opposite direction."

We undermine our innate wisdom by believing in what is true for others and by believing in what others judge is true of us. Beginning at home and at school, we learn through judgment and grading that we are good or not good at something. I always got C marks in art classes, leading me to believe I had no artistic talent. Only now in my adult life am I undoing that debilitating system and discovering my true artistic gifts.

> Believe nothing because a wise man said it,
> Believe nothing because it is generally held.
> Believe nothing because it is written.
> Believe nothing because it is said to be divine.
> Believe nothing because someone else believes it.
> But believe only what you yourself judge to be true.
> —The Buddha

The truth is that each of us is a product of eons and eons of evolution. We have learned and stored in our genetic history countless abilities. We are gifted far beyond our beliefs. According to the University of Iowa neurological study of intuition, it is in the emotional memory part of the brain that our intuitiveness resides, and so in recording everything, the intuitive brain has great know-how acquired through the vast experience of our collective heritage and individual experience.

> "When you truly possess all that you have been and done, which may take some time, you are fierce with reality."   —Florida Scott Maxwell

It Takes Guts to Follow Your Gut

In these times of change and even chaos, every decision is a risk. It is truer now than ever that successful people are risk-takers. Intuitive decision-making can be a scary proposition, for it often defies conventional logic. For Jim Adamson, the founder of the enormously successful Gap clothing company, to initially order 50,000 jeans instead of the planned, safe, and logical 5,000, was an intuitive jump, a courageous act of trust.[6] Following your gut in business gives you the entrepreneurial advantage of leaping over the mass of sheep who go along to only get along.

Here is another true short story. There was once a businessman who was tempted to buy in the 1950s what was then a novelty, a fast-food hamburger stand. He called in his expert consultants who told him to forget it; it was not worth the price. But as Ray Kroc put it, he felt something in his funny bone, so he bought it anyway. It is known today as McDonald's.[7] It just sold its 100 billionth burger.

Be Present

> "To win, you must be present."
> —Sign above a bingo parlor door

Intuition includes all the latest, up-to-date data we are aware of, and will respond in kind when asked. Intuition is thus always changing, mirroring the changes that are taking place. The more experience you have at anything, the more correct your intuition will be. But watch out for becoming the "expert," one who has become anti-intuitive, knowing how things used to be done and thus reliant on logic and analysis. The logical, analytical mind is too linear and too slow to be current. Intuition is in the now of life, where you must be in our changing world to be flexible—or flex-able, to be change-able, and adapt-able. It has been said that, "The past is history, the future is mystery, the present is a present. . . the gift of being in the now." Receive the present as a present, open it and use it.

The Middle Way

As intuition is a feeling, it helps to be emotionally balanced. Nothing skews accurate perception so much as lack of balance. Many of us are fear driven and so our intuition is a projection of fear, thus creating a worst-case analysis or perhaps, because of the fear, denying what is true. Others are desire driven, and so their intuition is a projection of what they only want to see. Either could in fact be the truth, but more often than not, the truth is somewhere in the middle. Some may say the glass is "half-empty" and others say it is "half-full"; truthfully and factually, the water is present to the midpoint of the glass.

Intuition Application: Bracketing the Truth

When looking at a situation, ask yourself: What am I AFRAID to see? Then ask yourself, What would I LOVE to see? Having thus bracketed your projections, in a state of inner PEACE and BALANCE, what do you see as the real truth?

The Wait-a-Minute Practice

Most of us are so much in our thinking head trying to get the right answer that we often ignore the intuitive feeling. Again, the single most difficult part of intuitive decision-making is being aware of the feeling. The feeling comes up so quickly that we don't even consciously acknowledge it. Keep asking yourself, "Wait a minute . . . what are my feelings telling me?" That conscious awareness of the feeling, without judgment (fair witnessing), enables your intuition to tell you how to correctly respond.

> "You can't be intuitive if you are trying to be right . . . . Wait for a few moments before allowing your mind to judge what's right for you."
> —Robert Cooper, *Executive EQ*

Getting Centered

> "No trumpets sound when the important decisions of our life are made. Destiny is made known silently."
> —Agnes de Mille

The "wait-a-minute" way to conscious intuition by feeling the original feeling is significantly enhanced by learning how to center yourself. Centering means coming to a balanced, open, aware state of being. You can do this sitting or standing so that you are aware of your breath coming from your belly, feeling the gravity on your sit bones or soles of your feet. In this state of balance, simply open into a vast emptiness of space and stillness, an open and clean slate. Without asserting or trying, allow the intuitive feeling in.

> "Instead of penetrating the mystery, we allow
> ourselves to be penetrated by the mystery."
> —Wendy Palmer, *The Intuitive Body*

This is essentially a "mindfulness" kind of meditation or contemplation. Though easy, because of our Western way of being trained to seek and go after the truth, it's not so familiar. In the mindful, intuitive way, we allow, accept, and receive, being nothing but an open container. This is why the receptive feminine energy and Eastern meditation techniques are so intuitive and valuable. We do not need to sit absolutely still or cross-legged for long periods of time, but it is a practice that needs to be practiced. The more you do it, the easier, quicker, and more seamlessly integrated into your life it becomes. This open, aware state can be achieved in a moment or a minute. It does not have to be divorced from the regular scheduling and busyness of life.

Be Quick!

As Lewis Platt, former CEO and president of Hewlett-Packard says, "It's not about the survival of the fittest, but about the survival of the quickest."[8] As the speed of business and life accelerates, only intuition can keep up with the decisions to be made from moment to moment. Platt calls intuition his "most valuable business tool," never taught to him in any business school.

By being quick, you don't have time to think, to get

into "paralysis through analysis." If you wait a minute to feel out the truth, you will still be faster than trying to logically figure it out.

Intuition Application: First Feeling

Ask yourself about a particular decision you need to make now. What is your first feeling in response? That is probably your answer. But ask yourself: How does that feeling feel? Trust it!

"If you wait, get in line."

There's No Formula

If you have been reading this closely, you may be confused by now. I argue to "wait a minute," but then "be quick." What to do? Intuitive people do not follow formulas and rules that must always be obeyed. We simply need to be ready to move fast—and slowly, depending upon which feels right at the time for the circumstance. Sometimes, the intuitive feeling is to take our time, and at other times, there's no need—it's clear, let's go!

I also write about getting centered, still and silent, and then I say, just start doing. Well, which one? Either one, depending upon your feeling at the time. Your intuition will tell you. We become unintuitive when we rely on strict directions for how to do things right. Be free to be you. Otherwise, we become like sheep, mechanical and monotonous.

"I once complained to my father that I didn't seem to be able to do things the same way other people

did. Dad's advice, 'Margo, don't be a sheep.
People hate sheep. They eat sheep.'"

—Margo Kaufman

Relax: Easy Does It

Intuition is a faculty that everyone has. Like a muscle, the more it is exercised, the stronger it becomes. The best way to work it out, however, is to take it easy. Pain does not equal gain in the intuitive fitness world. Don't try hard, don't think hard, don't be hard. Easy does it. Allow intuition to flow forth like a natural spring. Be open, receptive, soft. Intuition is the real soft, software of our times.

The great photographer Imogen Cunningham, who revolutionized the art, did it, according to *New York Times* critic Hilton Kramer, by "empathy rather than aesthetic invention guiding her eye and her lens to her most powerful images. . . and we get a sense of her own generous response to life."

The Body Knows. . . The Body Tells

"The body says what words cannot."

—Martha Graham

Your body will tell you every time what you are truly feeling intuitively. But you must, by experience, determine what certain physical indications mean to you. We are all different.

Literally, your gut may give you the answer. The ancient Chinese believed that wisdom resides in the stomach. If your stomach becomes nervous, pay attention. A chill up and down the spine will be a warning to some and a yes to others. A tingly or warm cozy feeling could be a go sign, whereas a heated sweat is possibly a no. Maybe your teeth will grind when faced with a certain event that you're just not comfortable with. Generally, illnesses, from headaches to heartaches, will tell you that you are on the wrong course, that something is not right. A stable, healthy physical condition indicates you're on your true course.

Just as you read other people's body language, let your own body talk to you. Perhaps crossing your legs and arms lets you know that you are intuitively closed or negative to an idea or situation. The way in which your mouth contorts and hands clasp may also signal something. Be aware of what your body does in any given situation, and you will know what your intuition is telling you.

> "I tried to learn, not from reason, but from my senses. But as soon as I began to study my perception, to look at my own experience, I found that there were different facts. There was a narrow focus which meant seeing life as if from blinkers and with the center of awareness in my head; and there was a wide focus which meant knowing with the whole of my body, a way of looking which quite altered my perception of whatever I saw. And I found that the narrow focus way was the way of reason. It was the wide focus way that made me happy."
> —Marion Milner, *A Life of One's Own*

Looking with the whole body is a way of perception that is comprehensive in taking in information. It leads to a whole-brain way of processing all different kinds of information simultaneously.

Intuition Application: Feel It in Your Body

Think of an undoubted truth in your life, for example, your love for a loved one. Where do you feel that truth in your body? Now, think to yourself the exact opposite: your total lack of love for that loved one. Where do you feel that untruth? Now you know where in your body you can intuitively feel your truth, and where in the body you can discern falsity.

Intuition Application: Feel Your Intuitive Power

Think of something you don't want to do. Where in your body is there a resistant feeling? Now think of something you sort of want to do, where does your body respond? For something that really turns you on, where do you feel it in your body? Now you know where to feel the intuitive truth for what really energizes and inspires you, and that is where you have your greatest power and possibility to succeed.

Truth Humming

What is a sound decision? What seems sound? Sound it out. If you want to hear your inner voice, give physical voice to what you are considering and evaluating. The most direct and effective way of sounding out the truth is to hum to yourself as you contemplate a situation or issue. Humming will enable you to physically feel your feelings and also get you out of your overthinking mind.

This sonic mirroring process is akin to how dolphins make assessments and decisions. They use a somewhat similar kind of intelligence, emanating a sonic vibration toward an object and receiving back a set of echolike vibrations that indicate its identity and nature. Listen to your own hum as it reflects your attention, it will speak to you.

Intuition Application: Hum the Truth

Take a decision you're weighing and evaluating. Imagine one of your choices in one hand and another choice in the other hand. Hum to yourself as you consider both possibilities. Let your hum sound out your soundest course of action.

Competition

In the heat of battle, our intuitions and instincts are unusually heightened. One great value of the emotional intuitive mind is that it's far quicker than the rational mind, and that it springs to action to help us survive in the competition of evolution. Intuition exists as our evolutionary intelligence; it protects our survival.

> "In evolution, this quickness revolved around that most basic decision, what to pay attention to, and, once vigilant while confronting another animal, making split-second decisions like, 'Do I eat this, or does it eat me?' Those organisms that had to pause too long to reflect on these answers were unlikely to have many progeny to pass on their slower-acting genes."
> —Daniel Goleman, *Emotional Intelligence*

The impetus of competition is why intuition is most useful and developed in the worlds of business, politics, dating, and sports. Use your competition as a way of arousing your own best intuitiveness.

Intuition Application: Sense Like an Animal

Ask yourself: What kind of animals are your competitors? What kind of animal do you need to be in order to survive and thrive among them? What kind of environment would be the most challenging to your animal competitor?

Gather Intelligence

One of the biggest problems in decision-making is information overload and complexity. How to make decisions when there is so much to consider? Scan. Scan the papers, the Internet, the word on the street, magazines in airports, overheard conversations, billboards. Intuition is not averse to information or to getting it from diverse sources. This is how Paul Fireman, founder of Reebock athletic shoes, began his fortune— by noticing the word "aerobic" and feeling there was something to it. In fact, intuition feeds on facts, opinions, stories, images, all sorts of seemingly unrelated stuff. It's all being stored in your subconscious.

> **"The mind of man is more intuitive than logical, and comprehends more than the rational mind can coordinate."**
> —**Vauvenargues, in *Forbes Magazine***

As Gertrude Stein once said, "Everybody gets so much information all day long that they lose their common sense." True. So, just take in all the info with an open mind, an open body, and an open heart and then let your intuition do the job. Your intuition is the information coordinator—it synthesizes and integrates everything and comes up with its verdict, by just a feeling. It's an amazing system, one that we have just begun to tap and that has been held back by antiquated beliefs and old science.

> "I get a *feel* for what I think is going on based on the information—not only the anecdotal information in the press and the statistical information assembled and compiled by the staff here, but also from the tone of the markets."
> —John P. LaWare, U.S. Federal Reserve Bank governor

Signs

> "A healer with a problem goes out into the forest, thinking about the patient, and tries to sniff out a solution by wandering, with an open mind, until something stops him, until a particular plant catches his attention and offers itself as a remedy. The trick is learning how to listen without censoring or getting in the way."
> —Lyall Watson, *Jacobson's Organ*

The intuitive person pays attention to signs—those meaningful "coincidences," like when you are thinking of someone and at that moment they call, or in the case of the shaman, the plant calls. Signs that give us direction seem to be not random accidents but synchronistic connections that occur astonishingly over time and space without any visible relationship. Just as radio and television transmissions are invisible to the eye and move through the airwaves of vibrational frequency, each of us is a transmitter of vibrations. Our movements, our voices, and even our thoughts are vibratory waves. It makes sense, then, that we transmit and receive occurrences that are on the same wavelength.

Sometimes these mysterious signs support our direction, whereas other times they may call into question our endeavor. The important thing is to be open to these events and allow your intuition to feel out what the sign is telling you. There are some, like the Native American shamans, who assign everything, from the weather to a baby's cry, as a message. The point is that this kind of observation and thinking triggers awareness of your intuition.

In truth, everything and every event in our lives is a synchronicity. It's all a message. As above, so below; the outer reflects the inner. The universe is one interconnected whole, so at any time and space, observe your world and see yourself. Look for signs. The other day I was evaluating my professional direction while sitting at the beach when a whale, on its way south to Mexico for the winter, fluked and showed itself. It came to me immediately that this was a sign, my intuition telling me to present to the world more of me, to have a bigger presence and identity. Telling you this personal story is a result of following that intuition.

Intuition Application: The Sign

For everything you have read, seen, and heard today, what single word, picture or happening stands out the most for you? How can that help your life or work?

Intuition Application: Signs of Synchronicity

Ask your intuition what the next physical event that happens to you means in terms of who you are or what you are doing.

Intuitive Thinking

> "We run this company not by the numbers, but on gut instinct."
> —Donna Karan, president of DKNY Clothing

Thinking comes in when we just don't have an immediate intuitive feel for the situation. In such cases, think out the options that could be right. Brainstorm. Then, choose the one that intuitively feels most true to you.

Except for mathematics, there are absolutely no true logical answers for anything. Ultimately, every decision we make is based upon a feeling of its correctness (in other words, upon an intuition). By understanding this, you will become more conscious of what you base your life on and far more aware of your intuition.

There is nothing more frustrating, however, than trying to justify a decision to another (and particularly to a chairman of the board, a supervisor, or group of your peers) by saying you just feel intuitively it's right. As Nancy Rosanoff writes in her book, *The Complete Idiot's*

Guide to Making Money Through Intuition, "Intuition will tell you what before why." In such mystifying cases, use your thinking mind to do the best you can to rationalize your intuition. It is through the thinking mind of words that we communicate and justify our intuitions, and even then it is an intuitive call of how to communicate—with what words, with what inflections, with what media, when, and to whom.

Waiting It Out

If no answer feels right and you are still confused about a given issue or situation, don't make a decision. Wait. Time is a helper.

Or make a decision anyway, and then give it a chance over a predetermined period of time for you to feel it out. In some Native American traditions one waits three days for a decision to prove itself or not.

Intuition Application: The Coin Flip

You can always try the "coin-flip" solution. Heads is one solution and tails is another. And you must commit to the decision. But, in fact, your reaction to the coin flip is your correct decision, not the coin flip itself. Try it.

If your intuitive feeling does not clearly and easily arise for you, let it be. You have seeded the intuitive subconscious for the answer to arise when it is naturally right. Relax.

The subconscious mind is the cooker where our ideas simmer while we are loafing. Newton was chillin' when he saw an apple fall and got the gravitation idea. Watt was relaxing in the kitchen when he saw steam lifting the top of the teakettle and conceived the idea of a steam engine. And there are plenty more examples of idea incubation by not thinking hard.

> "Many times we will get more and better ideas in two hours of creative loafing than in eight hours at a desk."
>
> —Wilfred A. Peterson

Resource Yourself: The Inner Advisors

The greatest resource in the world is you. It's not money, property, or connections. Inside each of us there exists a team of experts, expert in how to conduct the "business of living." In this new age, we are all engaged in what I call "youbiz;" each of us is being called upon to do it all. As we are products of eons and eons of genetic wisdom, we have only to access this vast repository of know-how. How? Our intuition is the doorway and clearinghouse for this wisdom to surface.

It's true that each of us is a small business unto ourselves. You, Inc. and Me, Inc. We are all businesses; we are all our own company. We are CEOs, making decisions and plans, and CFOs, budgeting and allocating time, money, and energy. As team members, we work with others; as consumers we buy; and as salesperson and marketer, we advertise and sell our services, ideas, and skills. As our own R&D division, we create. As entrepreneurs, we compete and take risks, juggle the finances and cash flow, learn from mistakes, solve problems, and scout out new ideas. Like COOs, we strive to manage efficiently, build and grow, protect, and produce.

We are also like entire governments unto ourselves, the state of You, the state of Me, guiding our own body politic. The legislature within us of different interests and voices gives us input into our various needs and desires; the executive within decides and acts; and our own inner court adjudicates conflicts and confusions.

Intuition naturally accesses these inherent abilities and roles that have been honed, seasoned, and recorded in the accumulated wisdom of our experiential memory bank. Our treasure box of know-how is rich, and intuition is our way of withdrawing from this endless fund.

Intuition Application: The Inner Advisors

To get a new idea, insight, or answer you may want about your business, first ask whose field of expertise does this belong to. For example, a financial question calls for the financier within, your own CFO. Close your eyes and imagine that advisor. Ask him or her questions—and trust the answers. It really is your own intuitive guidance. For a question about sales, ask your inner sales and marketing expert. Make a checklist of the functions and roles every business must have. Have it in front of you to remind yourself to find the appropriate intuitive mentor within. And don't forget to include one of your greatest business advisors—the consumer. Always, always ask your inner client what they feel you must do.

You may find that having one inner business sage works best for you. This inner guide may have all the answers you need for all your business questions and issues. The point is to get in touch with these inner advisors. This process works for any area of your life. For relationships, ask your inner love advisor, or inner child-care advisor, or inner work partner. Or simply ask your intuition what the other person is feeling and how they would like to communicate.

The Correct Decision

Not every intuitive decision you make will be the right choice from an outside point of view. Being 100 percent *right* does not happen, but 100 percent *correct* does if your choice comes from your heart of hearts. And if you follow the feelings that give you the greatest positive charge of energy, then, at the very least, you are utilizing all of your inner resources with utmost conviction and, therefore, giving yourself the greatest chance to succeed. When following your intuition, you are in your own place of power. Intuition is personal, and that is why it works for you. But remember, what is correct for you, may not be for another.

INTUITIVE ACTION

SURVIVAL OF THE ACTIVIST

> **"A vision without action is an hallucination."**
> **—Ancient Japanese Proverb**

One of the greatest barriers to a successful business of life is to be "caught by thought." Sitting and thinking can get you more confused and confounded than ever, let alone cause you to allow an opportunity to pass you by while you think about it. Get out of your head and into action. As the prolific genius, Buckminster Fuller, once said, "I call intuition cosmic fishing. You feel a nibble, then you've got to hook the fish." Intuitive people are activists. They get a lot more done than the "thinksters." We have so much to do in our lives, and intuition gives us the impetus and tool for getting it done.

> **"A man will wait for a long time with his mouth**
> **open before a roast duck flies in."**
> **—Ancient Chinese Proverb**

In this age of abundant opportunity, the dictum of "fire, aim, ready," works. We don't know what's going to happen anyway, so just do it. More importantly, in the doing, something useful, an unforeseen opportunity, will come forth. An example of this is NASA's space explorations. By going for it, at least 30,000 and counting new products have emerged. The world is built by spin-offs that happen by action.

Because intuition is a feeling, it's charged energy, an emotion that puts us into motion. Repression of our intuitive feelings and emotions is one of our greatest self-violations, a self-abnegation that kills the very life force of creation.

Intuitiveness is always reinforced and matured by attention to it and, even more strongly, by immediate action on it. There is nothing so enlivening and self-affirming as results, completions, and payoffs. Such outcomes are produced by intuitive proaction.

> "I find the great thing in this world is not so much where we stand as in what direction we are moving. To reach the port of heaven, we must sail sometimes with the wind and sometimes against it—but sail we must, and not drift, nor lie at anchor."
>
> **—Oliver Wendell Holmes**

Intuitions are activated while doing. Intuitive insight is inextricably tied to our "kinesthetic intelligence." Move the body and you move the mind. Action always brings out spontaneous "ahas!" that could not be preplanned.

Novelist Robert B. Parker, author of thirty books and best known for his *Spenser for Hire* series of television mysteries, questioned on how he writes, says that he "just feels his way around. . . . As a matter of fact I don't have ideas, I do this (mimes typing). . . I don't know what's going to happen. . . . It's a process I cannot articulate. . . . What I do is not intellectual."

Get going and get the answers. Feel it and do it! And do it *now!* Act with urgency, with immediacy. Then you act with inspiration and energy, full on with all your power and faculties, not depleted by the reservations and thought-up hesitancies of the analytical mind. That is what it takes in our modern world to succeed. As the philosopher and writer Ralph Waldo Emerson said, "Success is ninety percent enthusiasm."

> "If not now, when?
> If not you, who?
> If not here, where?"
> —Anonymous

It's OK to Be Slow

> "We cannot do great things on this earth. We can
> only do small things with great love."
> —Mother Teresa

In the movie *What About Bob?* a therapist, played by actor Richard Dreyfus, extols the virtue of taking "baby steps." I agree with that philosophy of "small and often." If we enjoy the process, as Mother Teresa obviously did, we act not just once but over and over again. Things get done by acting again and again, for every "again" is a gain, a gain. . . until completion. Robert B. Parker writes only five pages a day, but every day! Slowly, slowly, little by little, action upon action.

The problem for many of us is that our vision is great and feels great, but we get intimidated and even exhausted by the very idea of doing it all. So, we don't act, and it does not happen. Another vision sabotaged.

Intuition Application: Remembering Again and Again

Remember to ask over and over again, "What does my intuition say?" How do you feel right now about your own intuition? What's the feeling?

It's OK to Be Wrong

> "You may be disappointed if you fail, but you are doomed if you don't try."
>
> —Beverly Sills

One of the great gifts of intuition is that it comes out of experience, naturally and without effort. Through exposure to the new and different, your intuition becomes "practiced." Intuition is a product of learning. So the quicker you make a decision and get a result, the swifter your intuition learns.

> "Mistakes are part of the dues that one pays for a full life."
>
> —Sophia Loren

Failure is a great, great teacher, and, as it is said, the quicker you get through failure, the quicker you get to success. So make the decision and act on it. Don't let your critical, reactive mind beat you up for mistakes and stop you from going ahead. Your intuition knows what to do in a positive, proactive way. Intuition is your ally that keeps you moving, growing, changing, and evolving, by processing setbacks into messages for future breakthroughs.

> "Our wisdom comes from our experience, and our experience comes from our foolishness."
> —Sacha Guitry

The ABC and Ds of Intuition

A mnemonic device for being actively intuitive is to remember that it's as simple as the ABCs.

A is for **Awareness** of the feeling.
B is for **Belief** in the feeling.
C is for **Courage** to act on the feeling.
D is for **Doing** it and doing it and doing it until it is second nature.

6

INTUITIVE INTENTION

THE POWER OF PURPOSE

> "It is emotional intelligence that motivates us to pursue our unique potential and purpose, and activates our innermost values and aspirations, transforming them from things we think about to what we live."
>
> —Robert K. Cooper and
> Ayman Sawaf in *Executive EQ*

Intuition is the voice within us of our combined feelings, thoughts, and sensations that comprise our core being. Core intuition reveals who we are, why we are, and what we are to do. Our personal life purpose comes through our intuition. Look deep inside yourself to determine your life intentions by asking your intuition what you truly want of your life. What in your heart is your driving passion for existence, that which moves and sustains you.

When you know, without a doubt, your core purpose, then you can manage your life from a place of inner surety and integrity. And integrity in our world of ever-shifting change is becoming ever more valued. Authenticity of being and doing is the prerequisite for true success and leadership, lasting relationships, and for real happiness. Personal honesty, trust, consistency, continuity, congruence, and realness cannot be questioned but only respected and sought after.

The so-called "new economy" of e-business collapsed so precipitously because, in a sense, it was not real. It was based upon a vision and a dream that was not being met in reality. Somehow, most of us suppressed the intuitive feeling that things were too good to be true. Our reality-based intuition was distorted and denied by the fabulous sums of money that kept flowing in. Intuition can be corrupted by greed. It takes a strong heart to stay true. The lesson is, however, that if we don't, we fall.

We are now in the "real economy" where real results are valued. Let us be real, digging down deep to the truth, even if it's not something we would like to see. Interestingly enough, the greatest stock market investor of our times, Warren Buffet, did not join the e-trade bandwagon. He simply could not see reasons for jumping on, and he trusted the feeling in his gut, in spite of everyone else's urgings. Being an "intuitive realist" is the safest and, in the long run, the most productive road to follow.

> "Just because we acquiesced to all the investment money from Wall Street does not mean that the business will work. We compromised our values for fickle opinions (Wall Street). Tune out the noise and focus on your core business. Honor your own value system, because the deeply personal elements make the work satisfying. When it doesn't feel right, there's a reason."
>
> —Bill Malloy, former CEO of Peapod, in *Fast Company,* February 2001

Integrity of intention gives us the rocklike foundation to stay the course and not crumble into pieces when things go awry or differently than expected. Our innermost intention never changes and never varies. In this transient, crossover period in human history, we need, more than ever, personal anchors for our personal and professional life; otherwise, we can easily steer off course. Reliability and stability increase in necessity and value during periods of flux and uncertainty. Our deepest intention is the perpetual flame of the life force. It's what inspires us, the fire in the belly that keeps us going with verve and gusto. We are moved from the inside out, and that passion of authentic purpose cannot be extinguished or violated. We are on and cannot be turned off.

Many of the dot-com workers who lost it all in the crash are still committed to their vision, and it's my feeling that this will carry them through the dark night into the eventual light again.

The important thing is that your core intuition of intention manifests across your life, your relations, and your work. When your life purpose is aligned with your profession and your people, you possess a sense of seamless unity, a synergy of wholeness that evokes and exponentially energizes all of our innate resources and vital skills for extraordinary living and uncommon success.

Our work and friends are sacred when they reflect the soul's destiny. Our inner and outer life becomes a marriage, a sanctified growing ground for ongoing development and evolution of self and society.

Sacred work gives meaning to the workplace, beyond just making money. This search for meaning requires introspection. Why am I here? What am I working for? Only in your heart can you find the right answers for yourself. Finding self-meaning brings fulfillment at the deepest levels of our being and arouses a spirit of aliveness that produces a cornucopia of prosperity, for it is the life force itself, the source of all.

Winners in life are those who persevere, endure, and keep going. Perseverers are those of us who are committed and stay committed to the essential intention. This is not difficult when the intention is the truth of our very being. The ability to persevere is based on continued adherence and focus on the avowed, genuine raison d'être that comes from deep within our center. In truth, we are our work, and staying authentic to ourselves, which is the real mission we are on, carries us through the dark nights and cold days we all encounter.

Intuition Application: Why? Why? Why? Why?

Ask your inner self what your work intention is. Then ask why is that? And then ask why is that? Keep asking why until you feel you've reached your innermost emotionally charged purpose that you know will never waver and vary—for it is you. How does that feel to you? What is the feeling of integrity and authenticity? Where is it located in your body? Now you will know what's not true for you, what's not in your integrity, and you will have a measuring basis for knowing yourself and your wisest intuitions.

7 INTUITIVE VISION

FORESIGHT EQUALS FORTUNE

> **"Action without planning is a nightmare."**
> **—Ancient Japanese Proverb**

In this world of continuous change, we must look ahead to stay ahead. While the intuitive feeling is our pilot of the present, intuitive vision is our forecaster and navigator of the future. Inside the human forebrain is the human genius to foresee. Inside our mind's eye we have the power of imagining the future.

Inner visioning is an intuitive precursor to thinking in words. Prediction is pre-diction—before words. Even the great Greek thinker and logician Aristotle knew that "the soul never thinks without a picture first."

In our prescience by this act of previewing, we are prepared. We have the option to prevent and preempt. What we see does not have to be. If we like what we see, however, we have the motivation and knowledge to help produce that possible reality into actuality. A forecast is thus not cast in stone but is subject to alteration by our perception and action.

Bruce Pandolfini, one of the world's great chess teachers, on teaching students how to preview and play the game in their heads, says, "We can all do it. We all have amazing capabilities. At first, playing the game in your head feels like work. Eventually it becomes intuition."[9]

Looking into the future from different perceptual viewpoints, we can see a variety of *potential* realities. We can see the *probable* future, what we view as most likely to happen, and we can imagine different *possible* futures. We can even look at the *paranoid* future, that which we have to fear—this is a favorite of Andy Grove, successful CEO of high-tech giant Intel. Finally, we can look at the *preferred passionate* future, that which we would love to see.

This preferred future is the most important one to picture. It is what keeps us competitive and on the leading edge because it gives us the power to create the future. To clearly see what we want gives us the impetus to live out our core intentions and tap our inherent talents and gifts. We cannot live and succeed without following the vision of our heart's desire. It says in the Bible that, "The people shall perish without a vision." I believe that.

Making the future is accomplished by creating self-fulfilling prophecies. My most graphic personal experience of a big self-fulfilling prophecy was when I was stricken with hepatitis in Nepal. For a month, I sat in a Tibetan Buddhist monastery and visualized my liver getting better. Without any medication other than the power of positive picturing, I walked out of the monastery cured.

The prophecies most attainable are, paradoxically, those that are big and far-ranging, those that compel us again and again. They must be heartfelt, full of passion and desire. It's your dream. Remember, only dreamers got to the moon.

To make that passionate future come true, we need a plan and strategy. But always remember the adage that, "The best way to make God laugh is tell him/her your plans." Physicists have a theory for that. It's called the Heisenberg Uncertainty Principle: "The mere act of observing something changes the nature of the thing observed." However, the power of previewing is that, having looked in advance, we have more information to make better choices and responses to change.

In our dynamic, revolutionary times, plans are always subject to change and thus can only help so much. Reporters for the *Harvard Business Review* recently discovered that 41 percent of the companies on the *Inc.* "500" list of the fastest growing companies in the United States had no initial business plan. And 26 percent of these companies were started with just a rudimentary, back-of-the-envelope type of plan.[10]

The real value of strategizing is the process itself; it makes us more aware of all the contingencies and simply better prepared to handle them when and if they arise on an intuitive day-to-day basis.

> "Our information-laden environments are changing so quickly that strategic planning, as it's normally talked about, can be dysfunctional. You have to rely on *intuition*. That's what people have been relying on anyway, but now it's part of what we talk about and try to plan for."
> —Michael Ray, *Creativity in Business*

Of course, it is in our human nature to plan; it's just that we must plan differently than in the past. Strategic planning often used to be a numbers-crunching kind of exercise. But, as Kenichi Ohmae writes in *The Mind of the Strategist: The Art of Japanese Business,* "Successful business strategies result not from rigorous analysis but from a particular state of mind. . . in insights that are beyond the reach of conscious analysis."

> "The sharp eye for detail which aided the cost accountants of the last fifty years is yielding to a softer focus as the static management environment yields to more fluid and chaotic scenarios, which characterize interactions of multiple events occurring much too quickly for a classic analytical approach."
> —Jagdish Parikh, in *Intuition: The New Frontier of Management*

Intuition Application:
Envisioning the Potential Realities

As you look into the probable future, what does your conventional wisdom see happening. Given the way trends are moving now, where are they likely to take you and your business?

As you peer into your most paranoid future, what would you not like to see? What are you afraid to see? What is your worst-case scenario?

As you view the possible futures, what surprises do you see? What outlandish, off-the-wall possibilities exist in your imagination?

Storytelling into Foretelling

> **"The universe is made up of stories, not of atoms."**
> **—Muriel Ruckeyser**

With these pictures, including your *passionate preferred* vision, create a story of your future. Storytelling is a tried and true way for evoking your intuition. I like using the universal and archetypal story called the "hero's journey" as a general structure. Each of us is on a hero's journey, a mythic voyage to the quest of our choice.

Intuition Application: Intuitive Storying

Describe the quest you are on or goal you want to achieve (passionate preferred vision). Ask yourself: What is your path of adventure from here to there? What are your fears and perceived demons (paranoid vision)? What are the outrageous characters and pathways you meet (possible visions)? What are the sacrifices, and what are your strengths and allies that will enable you to leap beyond the conventional way (probable vision)? What does your intuition say are the immediate actions to take for each of these elements of the story? Make up a story of these classic features of success. Tell the story to your partner or your team, and have it told back to you. How does it sound, how does it feel, how does it look?

One of the great values of making up your future by a picture story is that you can remember it, and it will inspire you. The power of the pictured story is supported by the factoid that 80 percent of Americans know their zodiac sign, while only 20 percent know their blood type. Why? Because zodiac signs have an image attached to them and a mythic story behind their meaning, whereas blood types are only letters, words, with nothing memorable or motivating in them.

Symbolize the Future

The wisdom within our subconscious is often projected to our conscious mind through picture symbols. An effective way of looking ahead is by seeing a symbol for the future in your mind's eye and then determining what your intuition says that it means. Picture symbols activate subconscious information into an intuitive idea.

Intuition Application: Image a Symbol

Just close your eyes and allow in whatever single image regarding the future comes to your inner sight. Trust your first pictorial impression and your immediate interpretation of it.

The Oracular Way

The technique of using an oracle, like that of using tarot cards, employs both storytelling, synchronicity, and symbols in an intuitive way. Having done these "readings" professionally for over twenty years, I know it works. By picking cards face down, we get out of our way of projecting what we would like to see. The cards are only indications of what could happen, and if we like what we see, we try to fulfill the prophecy with action; if we don't like our cards, we determine how to best adjust to their possibility or even prevent their indications. The cards, laid out, present a picture story in symbols of what's probable and possible. It's critical to emphasize that such readings of the cards only give us information about the future, and it's our intuition, catalyzed by the cards, that responds in the correct manner for us. The tarot is only a tool for preview, not a prediction cast in stone. With this in mind, it's a great process that I heartily recommend.

Backcasting

Here is another intuitive way of planning by foresight. Sometimes we can't get from here to there, but we can get from there to here. NASA did this in their planning to get the first man to the moon. They started with his successful return and then continued with each step that preceded it.

Intuition Application: The Interview

A great intuitive way to backcast is to have somebody interview you, asking you questions about how you succeeded to your goal, starting from the achievement and working backward.

Extrasensory Knowing

"Sniff with your wisdom nose and get clear"
—Rumi

Searching out opportunities and looking out for pitfalls is like being a cat on the hunt. We talk a lot about visualizing, but what about the other senses of smelling, feeling, tasting, and hearing. Use your senses, but in a "metasensory" way. This is an amazing intuitive technique, and it works like this: Use your nose to smell out a particular situation. Not literally smell it, but if you were to give that situation a smell, what would it be? Senses and intuition are close cousins. When used in this way, our animal sense instincts bring us to our extrasensory perception (ESP), our sixth sense.

> **"I choose people with my nose. . . what else is there?"**
> —**Paul Fentener van Vlissingen,**
> **CEO of SHV Holdings**

Another way of metasensing the truth is to feel it out. In the ancient world, the priestesses who foretold the future were associated with the snake. Snakes are great heat detectors, and they strike where it is warm. Those seers of yesteryear would feel the temperature of the truth, what felt hot and what felt cold.

> **"It is not more light that is needed in the world, it is more warmth. We will not die of darkness, but of cold."**
> —**Jenny Read**

A tried and true way of knowing the truth of anything is to sense through the attributes of an animal. Indigenous shamans would take on in their imagination the quality of a jaguar or a falcon or a dolphin to ascertain things.

76

"Several years ago, while visiting the office of the CEO of a large Silicon Valley corporation, I saw a formidable Eagle fetish on the man's desk. He said that 'I use it whenever I am trying to develop long-term plans. It tells me a lot; you'd be surprised.'"

—Hal Zina Bennett, *Zuni Fetishes*

8 INTUITIVE INNOVATION

CREATE, CREATE, CREATE!

> "The heart is the origin of creative impulses. . . .
> Everything is tested internally, sifted, and sorted,
> gold from dross."
> —Julia Cameron, *The Vein of Gold*

There is an ancient wisdom that says, "Those who create the future, profit most by it!" The best way to succeed in today's business of living is to create yourself anew and to create new ideas, create new products, create new services. "New and improved" is essential to keep up with the world and with the competition. "New and different" gives you a unique market niche that stands out. "New and first" guarantees you a place in this survival-of-the-quickest world. *Since 1980, the number of new products launched each year has tripled and shows no signs of abating.*

Fortunately, creativity is a free resource that levels the playing field. You don't have to be a mental genius to be innovative. Everyone is creative through his or her own natural intuition. But innovation demands novel ways of tapping the genius of the intuitive subconscious.

> **"A hunch is creativity trying to tell you something."**
> **—Frank Capra, film director**

78 Whether it's creating a new product, a new process, a new relationship, a new you, or a new anything, intuition is necessary. In fact, eighty-two of ninety-three Nobel Science Award winners in a sixteen-year study declared that intuition is what led them to their discovery.[11] If you have a feeling about a new way, follow it. If something feels curious or interesting or exciting to you, pursue it! It's the way things get invented, through adventures of the mind—"inventure." I love what Jonas Salk, the developer of the Salk vaccine for polio once said: "It is always with excitement that I wake up in the morning wondering what my intuition will toss up to me like gifts from the sea. I work with it, rely on it, it's my partner."

It was recently reported in the *Wall Street Journal* that DuPont, through courses in intuition development, began to experience "one hundred percent increases in productivity." The time it took to develop new product lines and make them commercially available dropped from three years to three months.[12]

> **"There is always a connection between the random thing you select and your problem—and your job is to find it. We humans are quite good at finding patterns and meaning in the world around us—even if none were intended. Whatever you find will add insight into your problem."**
> **—Roger Von Oech, *A Whack on the Side of the Head***

For a new idea or a new insight about anything, pick at random a current event in life, or even an object in your office or on the road—what idea is sparked in you?

Metaphoric Magic

> "The metaphor is probably the most fertile power possessed by man."
> —José Ortega y Gasset, philosopher

I use a set of creative intuition cards called Voyager Tarot that I have designed for the business of living. These cards, through their symbols and meanings organized as a holistic way for being successful, provide new and different "ahas!" And they are picked face down, so in the surprise, the process takes us out of our preconceived and habitual ways of thinking.

Once, a CEO consulted me about how to create greater company profits. He happened to select the card called "Love." "What's love got to do with it?" he exclaimed, as visions of Tina Turner danced before our eyes. "This is how creative insight works," I responded. "Just be open, play with the concept and images." That led to his breakthrough of seeing that if he were to pay attention to the emotional needs and desires of his employees so that they would honestly enjoy their work, they would be more productive, and the company, in turn, would be more profitable.

> "The imaginative faculties are set in motion by
> the mental metaphor. Metaphor shifts the
> discourse, not gradually, but with a vengeance.
> You see what no one had seen before."
> —Roald Hoffmann

Vague Play

> "It's kind of fun to do the impossible."
> —Walt Disney

When Albert Einstein was stymied by some mathematical or theoretical problem, he would engage in what he called "vague play." He would walk around rather aimlessly and allow different feelings, signs, and images to come into play during this time. This activity excited his intuition to come up with new and different solutions. Einstein, in fact, attributed his scientific prowess to this process.

Intuition Application: Get New Ideas

Consider an issue for which you would like some new ideas. Go for a walk and play with whatever comes into your consciousness. Ask yourself, gently, what applicability any of this might have to your situation.

Laughter

> "At the height of laughter, the universe is flung
> into a kaleidoscope of new possibilities."
> —Jean Houston, *The Possible Human*

Don't forget to enjoy this creative playtime. Play is fun. Laugh! A sense of humor is like an extra sense, a sense that I have always found enormously useful in the creativity process. Did you know that babies laugh up to 500 times a day, and they keep investigating, creating, and growing. When we are having fun, laughing and playing around, we tap the natural and magical genius of the child within us.

> "Walling oneself off from the child's unconscious happens at great cost. This is where the abilities to play, fantasize, imagine, dream, laugh, and be spontaneous and crazy actually live. This is where real brilliant ideas are located. . . where 99% of our potential genius lies."
> —George Land, *Breakthrough and Beyond*

Imagine That. . .

> "I shut my eyes in order to see."
> —Paul Gauguin

"Imagination is more important than knowledge," declared Albert Einstein. By visualizing a man surfing a ray of light, he proposed the law of relativity. "Intuitively, it seemed clear to me that, judged by such an observer (i.e., the light beam traveler), everything should follow the same laws as for a stationary observer."

Imagination is an image that comes out of your intuition from your subconscious. Get the picture and then get the idea. What do you want to create? See it in your imagination. Then you have the magic of creation. The root word for image, imagination, and magic is *mag*, which means "power." And everybody has this power—imagination is free and natural.

> **"The truly valuable thing is intuition."**
> —Albert Einstein

The Art of Creative Thinking

Current studies of genius show that it can be characterized by the ability to merge disparate ideas, unrelated fields, novel combinations, and diverse disciplines into art.[13] When you want any kind of creative solution to an issue or a problem, look outside your field—perhaps into a field of poppies, a field "beyond right and wrong," a "field of dreams."

> **"A pioneer scientist must have a vivid intuitive imagination, for new ideas are not generated by deduction, but by artistically creative imagination."**
> —Max Planck

Several years ago I was looking for some advice about a particular issue. At random, a tree caught my attention, and in a flash, I saw how Mother Nature has all the answers. Want to grow yourself, your business, your partnership? Follow the growth principles of a tree.

In writing up my observations, I intuitively began to write in poetry rather than in prose. And then I composed a tree collage on paper while I was humming and singing.

This form of poetic/picture/sound thinking combined with the symbolic connection of nature and business gave me a quality of insight I had never before experienced. Perhaps, the greatest outcome of this serendipitous event was the creation of a new product of Wild Cards and book called *The Nature of Success.* The project began "at random"; it felt exciting and it felt right. Intuition had done its job, but I had done my job in following up on it and taking action.

> **"There is a poem at the heart of all things."**
> **—Wallace Stevens**

> **"Because vibration is the fundamental substance of everything, humming is a means of inner guidance, directing us with 'feeling' below rational thought."**
> **—Elisa Lodge, *Emotional Fitness: Energetic Workouts with Soul***

Dream On

> **"The problem is not finding melodies, it's, when getting up in the morning and getting out of bed, not stepping on them."**
> **—Johann Sebastian Bach**

One of the most potent ways to get creative insight is through dreaming. In 1865, F. A. Kekule intuited the shape of the ringlike benzene molecule by dreaming of a snake biting its tail. Robert Louis Stevenson attributed his books to the little people he called the "brownies" who directed his dream world. He said, "They do one-half of my work while I am fast asleep." Canadian physician Frederick Grant Banting found his laboratory procedure for the mass production of insulin through a dream.

Intuition Application: Dream It Up

For a problem or obstacle you have confronted, deliberately ask your subconscious to give you a dream. Let the events, people, places, and things in the dream act as symbols that suggest answers to you.

> "Nothing happens unless first a dream."
> —Carl Sandburg

The Saboteur of Creativity

Our critical beliefs about ourselves and our dreams block our intuitive creativity. We all have an inner judge who criticizes us. This is judgment we have learned from our society, our schools, our parents, and their parents. It is deep in our psyche, and it goes way back in time. Thus, we tend to discount our imagination as just another dream, a fantasy illusion. These self-doubts are programmed into our belief system. It's vital to recognize that the inner voice that says, "I can't," is actually coming from outside of us.

Intuitions are not, however, beliefs. They are positive, proactive, and productive, and they tap into the vast wellspring of our natural human genius.

Intuition Application: Befriending the Inner Critic

What is something you would love to create? What is stopping you from doing it? What belief is actually saying that you can't, or that you don't have enough time, or enough energy, or enough of whatever? Where did you learn that? Where does that belief come from?

The next time you hear yourself saying you "can't," say hello to this old belief and recognize it as a signal to proceed. And again, you never know what great things might simply come out of trying and beginning.

> **"An essential aspect of creativity is not being afraid to fail."**
>
> —Dr. Edwin Land

If you haven't failed, you haven't tried. Actually, if you look at failure, there is always success within it. At the very least, you will see what does not work and that intuitively leads you to the truth of what does. Science always gets its right answers through its wrong answers. Be like a scientist—experiment, explore, inventure.

Innovation Is an Inside Job

The most creative people are those who know and value themselves. Intuition is your authentic self. Learn to discern between what is true to you and what is coming from outside of you through societal conditioning.

The Latin word for intuition is *intueri*, and it means to look inside. Only when something originates within you are you original. Our natural genius comes out when we are being ourselves.

Innovative people work from the inside out. They are inner directed. The inner dimension is where the source work gets done. Creative visionaries always have the strength of their own conviction. They are self-led and self-created.

When It's in the Air, It's in the Air

Although originality is the result of self-authorship, it's just as important to realize that nothing is created in isolation. Whatever new ideas or visions you may come up with, once they have been thought, they have moved out into the airwaves for anyone else to pick up through their extrasensory intuitive antennae. This is why so many discoveries are made simultaneously at opposite ends of the world unbeknownst to the parties involved. This phenomenon is supported by the new quantum physics, by Bell's theorem that there is a connection between you and everything and everybody in the world, and by Rupert Sheldrake's morphogenic field theory that there exists morphic resonance of a communication across space and time via vibratory force fields between similar biological structures or thoughts. Therefore, it behooves you to act quickly on an idea, for someone else may have it as well.

> "There is one common flow, one common
> breathing, all things are in sympathy."
> —Hippocrates

The Ritual of Results

> "Some people have ideas. A few carry them into
> the world of action and make them happen. These
> are the innovators."
> —Andrew Mercer

I absolutely believe in what Michelangelo, the great Italian Renaissance artist, said of his creative process:

"I see the angel in the stone, and I chisel and I chisel and I chisel, until she is set free." To create, we need to act on our imagination and have a repetitive process for remembering our vision and goals, which can get lost in the mix of our busy and changing life. Here is a quick ritual that, if you repeat daily, will greatly help you in creating what you want, whether it be a new product, more success, a new job, more money, more time off, whatever. It takes repetition, a zenlike attitude of "chop wood, carry water" to make innovative things happen. Every day, work on your vision!

Intuition Application: Daily Ritual of Results

1. Remember the feeling. What is it that you really want? Feel it!
2. With your inner mind's eye, see yourself getting it. Visualize your goal attained with clarity and light.
3. Remember your know-how, your life experience, and inner experts for achieving what you want. And remember the inner critic, the negative beliefs that block you.
4. Act on the feeling, the vision, the skills—do it!
5. Keep repeating this process daily. My mantra for the new millennium is "make it up," today and tomorrow and tomorrow.

If you do this ritual every day, you will achieve.

9 INTUITIVE COMMUNICATION

THE NEW WAY OF RELATING

> "We need all of us out there, stating, clarifying, discussing, modeling, filling all of space with the messages we care about. If we do that, energy fields develop and with them, their wondrous capacity to bring energy into form."
> — Margaret Wheatley, *Leadership and the New Science*

The lifeblood of the twenty-first century is communication. Partnering, networking, teaming, collaborating, allying, and synergizing have all grown exponentially in this relationship world of ours. As always, the business of life is about people and the ability to get along and work along, but never before in human history have we experienced this variety, complexity, and volume of interactions. Count up your own partnerships of all kinds and you will be amazed.

The real revolution in our relationships is how we conduct them. The old style, associated with the patriarchal family and corporate hierarchy, is being replaced by a more consensual, equality mode. The critical, aloof, analytical, and ego-centered ways of communicating are giving way to a more open, respectful, and heartfelt process. Intuition plays the central role in our new way of relating because of its inherent qualities of empathy, sensitivity, respect, sincerity, openness and supportiveness.

Empathy

"Listen. Make a way for yourself inside yourself."
—Rumi

The new communication rests on the empathic ability to feel what another is feeling. Without this empathy, there is no basis for community or communication. To truly communicate means to actually know who another is, to be able to step into another's shoes—into another's heart. This is done by intuition, a feeling about that person's feelings. Communication is not talking at, but feeling with.

Such communication involves active listening, meaning to not analyze another as they talk and to enter into their field of feeling and mindset. The easiest way to do this is by mirroring them, by reflecting their own way of speech, facial mannerisms, and body language. Then the other person also feels comfortable with you and will in turn communicate more openly and honestly.

Sensitivity: Reading Others

Life and business is all about people, but sometimes we forget that. We get lost in the hype and idea of something great and are then sabotaged by the wrong people in the wrong place. Reading people is paramount to success. A businesswoman friend of mine introduced her plan and product line to a large corporation that had a great track record and reputation. During their initial meetings, she felt the proverbial "bad vibes" from their chief attorney and dealmaker. However, she put that aside and went on with the negotiations for another six months, only to find that the company cut her out and stole her proposal. The lesson she learned was: "Trust what you know to be true, and follow it."

As you empathically listen and mirror the other person, you will intuitively pick up cues and clues that further explain how they really feel. Intuition is sensitive, continually sensing and reading below the words and between the lines. What does a person's voice say? Listen and intuit. What do a person's gestures indicate? Watch and intuit.

In a recent study, people who are aphasics (unable to understand spoken language) scored significantly higher than others in reading whether a person was telling the truth or not. Their ability was based on their observations of a person's physical mannerisms as they talked.[14] Another study concluded that looking at a person's gestures from the eyes on up was more telling than any other part of the face.[15]

Personalities are colorful and can be read accordingly. A negative person could be drab or dark, a fun person yellow, a creative person green, a spiritual person indigo. These auras change, of course, depending upon a person's mood. It's possible to understand another, or even a group energy, by intuitively ascribing a color to them.

Once, in giving a presentation to a sales organization, I intuitively saw, beforehand, that they would be a "yellow and pink" group. It turned out that their brochure was yellow, meaning bright and noticeable, as sales people must be. But during the talk, I felt they were a red, rather than pink, crowd. My judgmental mind felt they were "too" red, but in the spirit of true communication, I let my voice and emotions rip, allowing my words to come out red—loud, passionate, and powerful. It worked.

Intuition Application: Aura Reading

Ask yourself what color impression you get from a person or group and what that tells you about them.

Respect

Intuitive communication is based on respect for others and their truth, having compassion for their situation and point of view, rather than being critically and negatively judgmental.

Intuition is a person's authenticity, so any time an individual is expressing their feelings, that is their truth, and that cannot be denied or denigrated.

Sincerity: Communicating to Commune

It is well documented how masterful women are as communicators. In one study, a variety of emotional dramas were filmed, and then the sound was turned off. Men and women were asked to determine what was happening in these scenes, and women scored significantly higher in their understanding in 75 percent of the cases.[16] Why? Because women communicate to commune: they want to feel and be with another, so they are empathic, active listeners and intuitive readers. Men, on the other hand, tend to communicate to get something— it's strategic, so their communication is often a game of one-upmanship, a competition that is anything but engaging and collaborative. In the business world of teams and partners, this traditional male style is counterproductive.

Ego: Get Over It

> "I have no sword;
> I make absence of self my sword."
> —Anonymous samurai, fourteenth century

Effective communicators who build a genuine sense of community must put their egos aside. Our ego is a defense for our fears and insecurities. The best communicators are those with a developed and secure sense of self, so there is nothing that must be protected. This is another reason why inner work—becoming aware of our fear and taking action to move through it—is essential for successful collaboration.

Often in my consulting work, I hear the same story: a supervisor or colleague being impossible to work with because of his or her demanding ego, which in the workplace is often masked by a person's mental smartness—absolutely no guarantee of their intuitive partnering ability.

Increasingly, formal business is organized around projects and is conducted by special project teams. The prime requisite for the success of any team, whether a business, a family or an athletic team, is a sense of unity, which is founded on the ability to communicate.

> **"The virtuoso in interpersonal skills is the corporate future."**
>
> —Shoshona Zuboff, *The Age of the Smart Machine*

Unity Through Difference

> **"Women are repeatedly accused of taking things personally. I cannot see any other honest way of taking them."**
>
> —Marya Mannes

By following the principles of intuitive communication, agreement is usually reached. Even when there are differences of opinion, they are respected and valued. Again, not everyone will have the same intuitive perception. This mutual airing and appreciation of everyone's personal feeling for the truth becomes the basis for incorporating and unifying multiple facets of the truth into a balanced, whole way of proceeding. Such an integrated plan of action transcends an exclusive focus which, instead of synergizing, is "unergizing"— an exponential decrease of energy through disunity.

It's a "Both/And" World

> **"You can't take sides when you know the earth is round."**
>
> —Patricia Sun

Old world, industrial-age hierarchical communication was based on an exclusive, either/or logic. The "adhochrichal" team approach of the information age synergizes differences by a "both/and" way of thinking. Rational logic does not serve this kind of diverse need. So, watch out for saying, "yes, but. . ." Rather, say, "yes and. . ." A higher and more common ground for agreement and unity will result.

A Sufi story: Two men had an argument, so they went to a judge for arbitration. The first man made his case persuasively and eloquently, and the judge declared, "That's right, that's right!" The second man then argued his case eloquently and persuasively, and the judge agreed, "That's right, that's right!" The clerk of the court upon hearing this exclaimed, "Judge, they both can't be right." And the judge responded, "That's right, that's right!"

The moral of the story is that everyone has a piece of the truth, and so it's really a question of finding a creative way that includes all versions. That's a solution.

The important element of team effectiveness is not just the agreed-upon inclusive strategy, however, but the willingness of all the team members to actively contribute. People and their motivation are more important than plans. Intuitive communication inherently engenders value for everyone's perceptual position and their feelings. In being heard, seen, understood, valued, and included, team members are more than likely to wholeheartedly participate.

The Circle: Shape of the New Culture

> "Everything the Power of the World does is done in a circle."
> —Black Elk, in *Black Elk Speaks*

Partnering no longer means a hierarchical, fixed, long-term incorporation but an interactive "adhocracy" of flexible, dynamic, co-creative project teams. Teaming up in this way naturally brings about ever-evolving and shifting circles of community. Circular partnering is consensual; the group arrives at decisions together. In this form of shared leadership, everyone is recognized and acknowledged. The circle is an open space for creativity and a safe place for acceptance. Personal intuitions and feelings are sought out. Circular strategizing is, in fact, a form of communication that inevitably produces an exponential growth of power that transcends the individual. It synergizes!

Synchronicity

I am sure that we have all experienced those moments when we are thinking of someone distant and, at that moment, they call. We call this synchronicity, a communication that transcends space in time. From the new physics, we now understand how this is possible. The implication is that much of our teamwork is conducted by this kind of invisible connection. And the more contact we have with another over time, the greater this synchronous communication becomes.

The point is to trust in what you are sensing of another team member's feelings. Whenever you receive any inner feelings of danger, conflict, or need for help, follow up on these with a physical conversation. Sometimes these intuitive communications occur during a dream; follow up.

The face-to-face, open space of the circle is not only symbolic it is actually conducive to this synchronous process, for a great deal of nonverbal communication flies back and forth across the open circle. When synchronicity is acknowledged as one of the vital mediums of team communication, it expedites work by quantum leaps!

The Intuitive Leader

> "Leaders learn to heed the voice within."
> —Stratford Sherman, in *Fortune Magazine*

As people are the most important resource in any business or organization, empowering them is the sine qua non of leadership. In corporate business, there is probably nothing that is given as much lip service as empowerment; hence, it has become an almost cynical cliché, but it is true, and it won't go away. The organization or person that gets it, wins—clear and simple.

The Steps of Empowerment

First, discern where the *passion* is. Your intuitive sensors will know when passion is sparked—the voice, body, everything becomes more animated. You can feel it. An energy vibration and aura is transmitted.

Then, let your intuition discern the fear that blocks the living of that passion. What does your intuition say is the action to take for moving through the fear? Little steps of action, action, action.

Only in action is fear transformed into confidence. And all the while, remember to affirm and reaffirm inherent strengths and virtues, always acknowledge improvement and every little success as specific goals are attained.

Some of the leaders most skilled at empowering are professional football coaches. Every week they must empower their teams under extremely competitive conditions. The most successful coaches are always saying and meaning, "You can do it, don't you love it! You're getting better, don't you love it!" It's passionate and positive, positive and passionate.

Empowerment ultimately means having the confidence to feel and act on one's own intuition. Only then are we fully responsible, and at that point, we are not only self-led, but leaders of others.

The ultimate goal of empowerment is to make yourself or another into a complete person—meaning a whole company in himself or herself—thus, acting as a total business: responsible for leading it, creating it, budgeting it, selling it, growing it. Everyone's name should have an "Inc." after it.

Empowerment is not just a bunch of empty, nice-sounding, "you can do it" platitudes. It includes critique—empathic, judicious feedback. With face-to-face sensitivity, positivity, and specificity, critiques can empower rather than denigrate and destroy. As a matter of fact, in one study, inept criticism was ahead of mistrust, personality struggles, and disputes over power and pay as the leading reason for job conflict and low morale.[17]

> "It is with the heart that one sees rightly; what is essential is invisible to the eye."
> —Antoine de Saint-Exupéry, *The Little Prince*

The Four Es of Leadership

This is a very easy and useful way for remembering the essentials of empowering communication. I learned it from a doctor friend of mine as a means for effectively healing patients. I use this process in all consulting, training, and public speaking.

1. *Engage* by finding a way for getting a person's open attention. A true story is often the best way to initiate rapport.
2. *Empathize* with a person's situation, feeling their feelings about it.
3. *Educate*, teach, train, mentor, coach the skills necessary to do the job.
4. *Enlist*—get a person to sign on and agree to carry out the counsel and education.

Great leaders intuitively follow the four Es in communicating.

They *empathize* by feeling the pulse of their people. They feel what others feel about their condition.

Leadership is based on truth, on the prevailing senti-
ment. Leaders walk in the shoes of those they lead.
They know what others want, what their aspirations
and hopes are.

Leaders *enlist* support by having a vision for getting
beyond the present situation to a commonly held vision
and dream. The power of creating an actual picture of
what we want in our hearts and minds cannot ever be
underestimated.

Effective leaders are intuitive visionaries, but they
must be grounded and practical enough for their people
to see the real possibility of getting to where they want
to go. All the motivational talk in the world will do nothing unless there is a doable plan for achieving the com-
pelling vision. This is part of the *education* process—
the how of it all.

To *enlist* participation in the plan, a leader must
show that *together* they can do it. They create a sense
of greater mission, a collective urgency, a drive that
even transcends their own individual and personal
lives. One of the reasons for the success of the dot-com
Silicon Valley business culture has been their sense of a
mission of transforming world consciousness through
the service of their technologies.

Leaders who do all of this are purely intuitive. They
haven't organized focus groups or taken polls for
researching people's needs and wants. They listen, they
feel, they imagine, they plan, they incorporate, they
emote, they act. No scientific study could determine
that Martin Luther King's vision of "I have a dream,"
would carry the day.

> "I could hear an inner voice saying to me, Martin
> Luther, stand up for righteousness. Stand up for
> justice. Stand up for the truth."
>> —Martin Luther King, Jr.

Quest and Questions

> "Have patience with everything unresolved in your
> heart and try to love the questions themselves. Live
> the questions now. Perhaps then, someday far in the
> future, you will gradually, without even noticing it,
> live your way into the answer."
>> —Rainer Maria Rilke, *Letters to a Young Poet*

Our questions lead us on our quest. Those who ask the
questions establish the quest and set the agenda.
What are the questions? That is the question.
Questions come from deep inside, from our curiosity,
our aspirations, our drive to evolve, survive, and thrive.
Questions are inherently intuitive, for they come from
the mysterious source of creation. I enjoy what Pablo
Picasso once said, "What good are computers, they
only give answers."

> "The ability to live in the question, rather than the
> drive for the answer, helps you keep your antennae
> up and eyes open."
>> —Leonard Pascale

Those who create the world and make the future are the
ones with the questions, for they are the leaders of the
quest. Perhaps the best way to empower, inspire, moti-
vate, and lead is by asking the right questions. The

answers to the questions come from inside, for answers are felt, and they reveal. In revelation, revolution begins. Intuition goes "intuaction." As Albert Einstein once said, "The formulation of the question is far more important than the answer." His questions led us to one of the most stunning and momentous revolutions in human history.

Intuition Application: The Leading Question

Leadership is based on the age-old inner quests of Who am I? Where am I now? What do I want? How do I get there? To be a leader, ask these questions of yourself. And ask yourself: Are your answers representative of the people you lead? Do you feel how they feel? Is your vision their vision? Is your plan in their understanding of the doable? Is your sense of mission their sense of mission?

Intuitive Sales and Marketing

Sales operate throughout all aspects of our lives. We need to sell ourselves, our ideas, not only our products and services. We sell to others when we empower, when we inspire to action, when we lead, when we enlist agreement and consensus.

The successful foundation for all these kinds of selling is communication—meaning, again, empathy, feeling intuitively what others are feeling. You get what you want, a sale, if you help others get what they want. Selling really works when you are truly of service to the aspirations and needs of others. Your intuition is an information sleuth, ferreting out what others feel they desire.

All people are intuitive, and we all base our decisions on a feeling that feels right for ourselves. And so for anyone to buy us, or what we are selling as an extension of ourselves, we or our products have to be perceived as creating a good feeling.

People buy a feeling that is primarily based upon a picture of how it's going to make them feel. This caveat must be understood—people think in images, not in words. So, present a picture of how it will feel to buy. Ask them to imagine what it would be like to have what you are offering. Effective selling is not hype, but true communication that establishes a sense of commonality or community.

My favorite illustration of this point is the study taken of 1,000 salespeople from seventy-five different American firms. The three characteristics of the top salespeople were the ability to answer objections, be properly groomed, and wear black shoes! And the three characteristics of the least successful salespeople were the ability to answer objections, be properly groomed, and wear black shoes![18] So, it's not about your dress, it's not about your mental agility, its about something else: trust, a belief in you by your customer or friend or partner that comes from honest communication, the ability to establish rapport, even relationship.

Sold on You

The absolute key to sales is being sold on yourself. All sales start with buying who you are. Customers, clients, and colleagues must buy you before they buy your services and your ideas. Selling is the effective communication of yourself. As selling is essentially a transference of feeling, you must feel good about yourself. If we have devalued ourselves, then everything we pitch will be devalued.

Intuition Application: Buy Yourself

What aspect of yourself are you not sold on? What action will you take to do something about it?

In just taking action to improve any aspect of your life, you feel better about yourself, and I guarantee this will positively impact on your marketing and marketability.

Effective sales result when you feel good about what you are offering. If you are to be convincing, you must be convinced. You must know inside yourself that you are telling the truth. Integrity pays off. As they say, "Believers are closers." Integrity in sales happens the more you become sold on yourself, for you cannot even buy yourself if you know that you are out of integrity.

Selling to the Four Personality Types

The standard psychological assessments currently being used in the business world today indicate that humans comprise four different personality types. Thus, a very helpful process of creating rapport is to use your intuition to determine the type of person you are trying to communicate with and sell to.

Some people are the type A "executive" in command, active personalities. How do you identify them? Look at their symbols: how they dress, what's in their office, how they talk, their pace of action. You can tell. How do you sell to these types? By letting them take the lead. Go along, but have practical ideas and solutions for why you or your products work.

Another type is the "thinker," who is a mental, logical, reflective personality. They want the facts, and the right facts. So be prepared, know your stuff, take your time, and don't push.

A third type is the "socializer," the butterfly that carries the gossip, the fun, the upbeat energy! I am sure you could picture one of these types in your mind right now. Have fun with the sales process, and don't talk sales right away. Talk about anything else of social value—trends, clothes, people, whatever. Let the business happen in due course.

The fourth type is the "teamworker," a harmonizing, empowering, people-oriented, quasi-therapist, caregiver type. They want to do good for all. Be sincere, come from your integrity, speak from your heart, look them in the eye, and show them how your services improve the quality of people's lives.

Know Yourself, Morph Yourself

To effectively relate to these four personality types, you must first know your own. Which one are you? That is your comfort zone, your inherent strength, and the kind of people you will naturally be most effective with. The really important thing, however, is to be able to take on any one of the four characteristics. Being able to shape-shift or morph yourself into being like your customer or colleague or boss is essential. And it's a way of developing all of yourself and all of your talents and resources. So, always, always, for all personality types, mirror them (without overmirroring). This basic principle of communication will get you everywhere.

Whenever I make a presentation to a group, I first intuit who they are. I get as much information as I can about them beforehand (remember, intuition feeds on information). If it's a group of CEOs, I call upon the CEO in me to know what they want and how to be in their presence. If it's a doctors and nurses group, I get into the healer/therapist in myself. A sales conference tends to be more social, so I loosen up, get my jokes and stories out.

Like a shaman shape-shifter, sometimes we have to be able to switch our presentation style quickly! Once, with a group of accountants, I was prepared to mirror a "thinker" personality type. Wrong. They were a young, raucous, irreverent dot-com accountant type crowd, so immediately I had to shift. Intuitive mirror work requires a chameleonlike flexibility and adaptiveness.

Metaphor Marketing

> "Everything we see hides something else we want to see."
> —René Magritte

To know how to market your goods and services is to know what makes customers feel good about them.

Traditionally this has been done by surveys and focus groups. But these methods do not access real feelings, which are buried deep in the subconscious. A new way, termed "metaphor marketing," is being developed. It asks the potential customer to select from magazines picture symbols that somehow represent their feelings about the product. Later, they explain verbally what the pictures mean.

It was out of this process that Motorola decided to call its new security system, "Watchdog," simply because of the large number of dog pictures selected about the product, representing the respondents' feeling that they wanted a loyal, protective friend. It has been marketed, thus, less as a technological tool than as a companion.[19]

10 INTUITIVE FITNESS

THE BODY SENSORIUM

> "By cultivating your kinesthetic wisdom, you can begin to unleash your own inner genius to help the mind and body work together as a seamless whole."
>
> —Howard Gardner, *Frames Of Mind: The Theory Of Multiple Intelligences*

Much of our intuitiveness is displayed in response to incoming information—a phone call, the look on a face, an e-mail, a conversation, an article, a situation, an assignment. Our physical body is the first to receive new messages, whether by hearing, seeing, or by any of the physical senses. Even the things we pick up telepathically by the sixth sense of ESP are vibrations that first enter through the body. Our bodies are sensoriums, with a variety of sensory antennae. The more acute our physical sensitivity, the sharper we are as receivers. Skilled intuitives have finely honed corporal intelligence.

The physical component of intuition is seldom emphasized, but it is the foundation for intuitive living. If, for example, intuition is like a message that goes through a wire or a cable, then the wire had better be effectively working. Our body is the wire, the channel, and conduit. Maintain it and improve it. For, if our bodies are clogged, overstuffed, frazzled, worn out, and wounded, like a faulty wire, messages won't get through.

The body knows. It registers, records, and responds to our feelings and thoughts. It even creates our emotions and states of mind. When our body is out of balance, our emotions and our intuitions are naturally out of balance, as well. Whether by improper diet, lack of rest and exercise, stress, or illness, an unhealthy body impedes and skews intuitive accuracy, creativity, and action.

I cannot stress enough the importance of physical health and fitness for the intuitive world we live in. Remember, how you see the world is how you are emotionally, mentally, and physically.

There is a deliberate and conscious way of staying intuitively sharp and physically healthy and energetic. I call it the "Intuitive Fitness Workout." You can do the workout as a routine or incorporate elements of it throughout your day.

The Intuitive Fitness Workout

> **"If I could tell you what it meant, there would be no point in dancing it."**
>
> — Isadora Duncan

The first principle is to *breathe*. We forget to breathe; I mean fully breathe. Native Hawaiians call white people "haoles," Polynesian for "without breath." It's an ironic trick that the secret to life is right under our nose, so obvious and so simple that we ignore it. Without oxygen we die; thus, the more we oxygenate the body, the more intelligent it is. Whenever you remember, inhale and exhale fresh air, big and long. Inhale from your stomach and run your breath all the way up through the chest and out through the crown of your head like a fountain of air. Exhale fully through your entire body. A wide-open mouth that eats the air is symbolic of the principle of openness, receptivity, inclusiveness, freshness, new-ness, energy. In a word—aliveness! *Now, as you breathe in, what comes to you, what do you see in your mind's eye to allow and bring into your life and work?*

The second step of the workout is to *stand up*. Got a decision to make and feeling stuck? Don't sit on it. Stand up! We get 20 percent more oxygen to the brain when we are standing than when we are sitting; it's a fact. And it's been noted that meetings go 20 percent quicker when held standing up.

When we stand in a breathing, grounded, flexible way, we are on our toes. In a state of alertness, we are in the intuitive way. We can move on things with speed. Sitting down is about thinking, taking time, and often putting off and procrastinating. Most likely we already have gotten the intuitive message about what to do, but our social conditioning and lack of self-trust have taught us to analyze and be tentative. Standing up is about being bold, being seen, taking steps, leading. Look at football coaches: in their fast-paced game, they have to be always on the ball, so they stand. They're on

the balls of their feet, alert to every situation and con-
tingency. *As you stand and breathe, what do you know
intuitively that you need to be alert to?*

The third principle of physical intuition is to *move*.
Intuition thrives on physical movement, for intuition,
itself, is always in motion. Life is in motion, and we have
to keep up. Change is a constant, and in movement we
live in accordance with this natural law of the universe.

The key to effective movement is to move with your
breath. In fact, let your breath be the prime mover,
directing your body's motions. Let the body go; release
it, and let it move wherever and however the breath
takes it. Movement without breath is lifeless, mechanical, robotic—everything that intuition and the intuitive
body is not.

As this is predominantly a water planet, and we are a
water body, our motions are meant to be fluid. And intuition is a flow, a never ending flow of feelings that move
seamlessly onward. Sometimes we freeze with fear as
our inner fluids run cold. In anger, our fluids are hot,
and we boil over. In surprise, we may pass water. In
laughter and sorrow, we shed tears. In getting sexually
turned on, we may get wet.

The starting point for fluid motion is bending your
knees. While standing, flex your knees so that you can
fluidly move. Do your intuitive workouts with your
knees bent to be flex-able and change-able. This will
give you endless support, agility, and bounce.

As you move the body, you will move the mind. Rigid
bodies lead to rigid ideas. Walk, wiggle, fidget, dance,

stretch. As it has been said, "Problems cannot be solved by the kind of thinking that got us into them," so try thinking in motion to find new ways, new solutions, and new answers. NASA studies of astronauts moving weightless in space have shown that a different quality of mentation results from "kinesthetic thinking." New thinking is active thinking and feeling thinking—an intuitive thinking that energizes our whole body intelligence. It has been estimated in a study by educator, Viktor Lowenfeld, that one-fourth of the population shows a clear preference for kinesthetic intelligence. I always go for a walk to get new ideas and perspectives, and as I am doing now, I write on a fluid, bouncy physio-ball to keep the intuitive ideas flowing and creative. *As you are moving, fluidly in synch with your breath, what comes to you about any changes and moves you need to make in life?*

The fourth principle is *sound out*. Each of us is a transmitter. Our bodies and minds, our thoughts, and our feelings are vibrations that emanate out into the world. And what you put out is what you bring in. In a way we are all sounding out, even in our silence, through the vibration of our very being. Thoughts, people, and situations come to us via our transmissions. When we put feelings, visions, and ideas out through our sounds—whether they be words, calls, cries, prayers, songs, grunts, or cheers—we are communicating. We extend ourselves to the community of life and free ourselves from our own internalized, isolated being. Sounding out is freeing! And intuition flows and grows in free and open conditions. We invite the wisdom and liberating newness of the dynamic outside world to renew us in the same way that oxygen does. By sounding out, we give ourselves space for fresh new feelings and thoughts to come in, just as by fully exhaling, we allow in new, life-giving breath.

A sounding out technique that I use to free up my voice to invoke the world of possibilities is to "move my vowels." With breath, sound out hey, hee, hii, hoo, huu, and keep going, sounding them out in a wavelike way: haaaaahaaaa, heyyeeeeehoohuuu. Combine, play, create, energize! *As you sound out now, by making any kind of wavy tone in coordination with breathing it out, what is it that you want to release and free up in your life? What new energy do you want to invite into your life?*

The thing to remember about the workout is to breathe, stand, move, and sound out with emotion. *Emote.* Intuitions are feelings, so we need to feel.

Humming

> "To befriend our feelings, we can dance them, sing them, act them. . . we can creatively explore and celebrate them."
>
> —Gabrielle Roth, *Maps To Ecstacy: Teachings Of An Urban Shaman*

If you truly want to know what you are feeling about anything, any person, any issue, any situation, give it a sound. The sound will reflect, audibly, your intuitive feeling. Try this by humming. The great thing about humming is that you can do it so softly that only you can hear (it works in the office or in situations with others around).

My own favorite way of sounding out is by humming. Humming is also the best way to enliven and attune the body instrument. It vibrates, awakens, massages, and heals your inner organs, bones, and outer muscle structure. It gets your motor running. Hum as though you were revving up your engine. *What do you need to get started in your life now?*

Intuition Application: Make Up a Hum

Make a hum about anybody you know. What does it tell you about your feelings toward them? Hum about a project or assignment you are working on. What does your hum say about how you feel about it?

Here are some other humming intuitive exercises. Hum from your heart (again, don't forget to move fluidly with breath as you do this). This hum mirrors your heart's desire. What does your hum tell you about what you want in life? Perhaps your heart hum is full of sorrow. Then what brings you sadness? Get it out by your hum. Now, hum deeply from your gut, your stomach. What does it tell you about the reality, the bottom-line truth about any situation? Now, hum in a high-pitched sound from the top of your head. What surprises and high adventures are signaled?

To become alert to an intuition of anger or fear that signals you to watch out and be careful, you can do the anger and fear hums. Hum in an angry way now; exhale your hum with force, maybe shake your fists and even stomp. What makes you angry and upset when you do this? Now, hum in a fearful manner, inhaling, tensing, and repelling your body backwards as you do so. What is your fear? Let the action of fear humming identify it.

You can reduce these humming sounds and movements to bare microsounds and micromoves, so that you become acutely aware of them.

To find your emotional center, where your deepest and truest intuitive wisdom resides, do the centering hum, breath, and movement. Move your arms in and out in coordination with your breath and humming so that your body is like an accordion. Do it slowly, fully, a few times. This naturally takes you to the truth, to your most intelligent inner knowing. As you do this, what does this state of neutrality and peace tell you?

Expressive Intelligence

A fascinating success story of moving the body and voice to move the mind and move the organization is the Danish hearing aid company Oticon. In the past several years, this company has introduced ten major product innovations, including the world's first digital hearing aid. Why? One major reason is that everyone there works at a mobile workstation, so employees are always on the move. As its leader, Lars Kolind says, "It's an environment that maximizes walking, talking, and acting."

Simply put, expressive people are feeling people.

The expressiveness of a Maria Callas or a singer like Joe Cocker or a Robin Williams is due to the feelings that are moving them. Move to your feelings, and feel with your movements. Talk with your hands. Think aloud. Hum. Dance out the solution. Jog your intuition. Laugh your way to the bank. Jump for joy. These simple little expressions will exponentialize your creative genius.

INTUITIVE ENERGY

THE BOUNDLESS FLOW OF RENEWAL

> "I love people. I love my family, my children. . . but inside myself is a place where I live all alone that's where you renew your springs that never dry up."
> —Pearl Buck

We all know that business and the business of living can be exhausting and deadening. It can literally kill us with heart attacks. It can bring on unhealthy addictions. So, the real personal bottom line is energy! I know energy is not a sexy word, but it's the truth. With energy we can keep up to speed, we can continue to change and reinvent, we can perform and produce. Indeed, health is wealth. Energy is "inner chi," the life force itself, the ultimate resource in the business of living.

It is not commonly understood that intuition is an energy source. It gives us the mental, emotional, and physical relief we desperately need because it is so effortless, quick, and natural. It allows us to rest while working and to be at peace while active. As an impulse that goes through our entire system, it releases within us a spark, a charge that stirs the heart, stimulates the mind, and moves the body.

A true intuition is one that energizes—feels right and feels good for our entire system and mobilizes us. Intuition keeps us going and going because it synergizes. By unifying all of our faculties into a single field of intention and action, all parts of our selves feed each other and create a greater energy. When we are fully and totally into what we are doing, a dynamic sense of unity results, and as we know, the whole is greater than the sum of the parts. As "team self," we are at our strongest.

Intuition Application: Synergize

When you have a major decision to make, remember to consult each and all parts of your self. Do a quick check-in—how do your mind, your heart, and your body feel? If they are not in agreement, then you are not prepared to make the decision. Let your intuition bring all of your parts together. When your whole self is in consensus, do it!

Time

So much of our fatigue is due to the long hours we spend in our working lives, and the statistics show that we are working longer now than ever before. Intuition speeds up our productivity. Intuitive decision-making is instantaneous, and if you put intuition into immediate action, things just get done more quickly.

When the opportunity of this twenty-first century life is to enjoy our leisure, it is a step backwards to be working even more. Time cannot be recovered. It is simply imperative to find a way of making shortcuts without sacrificing quality and lofty goals. The intuitive way leaps over conventional timelines and even time management programs because it is not linear in time, but circular, ad hoc, and seemingly random.

Flow: A New Way of Working

When you look at it, the business of living today is messy, disorderly, chaotic, slowfast. Trying to organize your business life in a straight line of time and activity does not always work. In the industrial age, assembly-line order worked, but not in the information age. Like a busy bee, just fly about, from this project to that phone call to this client; going where you feel like going, where it feels good, and where you feel you must when it's imperative. In fact, there are no straight lines in the universe, so take a circular, crooked course and go with the flow of your feelings, which will put you in synch with the laws of physics. If it feels good, do it!

This intuitive flow way of working may seem inefficient, but only because we are so accustomed to perceiving productivity in terms of the mechanical, linear model. When we circulate about in accord with the intuitive spark, we have more energy and produce more—and in less time!

Unlike the machinist of the industrial age, the information-age knowledge worker is artistic. Like an artist moving from one painting to another, go to where the energy and inspiration is. Keep circulating. Circulation is health.

Time-out for Time Within

> "If your mind is empty, it is always ready for
> anything; it is open to everything. In the beginner's
> mind there are many possibilities; in the expert's
> mind there are few."
> —Shunryu Suzuki, *Zen Mind, Beginner's Mind*

If you don't know what to do or how to do it or are just plain tired, take a break. Although intuition is always on, it will tell you to rest. In the intuitive flow way of working, taking time-out can take you time ahead. Take time to do nothing, for in the open void, the screen and filter of our perception is wiped clear and clean. In the blank space of nothing, new and renewed impulses and inspirations can come in. Time-out can mean anything from an extended sabbatical to a one-minute closing of the eyes and ears.

Meditation will be of great benefit to your intuitive acuity. Not only does it refresh but it also puts you in the mode of going within and listening within for solutions and direction. You become sensitive in your silence to how your intuition likes to signal and speak to you.

> "In silence, we often say, we can hear ourselves think;
> but what is truer to say is that in silence we can hear
> ourselves not think, and so sink below our selves into a
> place far deeper than mere thought allows."
> —Pico Iyer

In the open void of silence, we are more capable of not only understanding our own inner truth but the truth of another. As Pico Iyer says, "In silence. . . we can hear someone else think."

To illustrate this point, there is a wonderful Sufi story by the poet Rumi.

> Shaikh Sar-razi was seated one day among his disciples. One of the disciples had a longing for some roasted sheep's head. The Shaikh signaled, saying, "You must bring him some roasted sheep's head."
>
> "How did you know that he wanted some roasted sheep's head?" the disciples asked.
>
> "Because it is now thirty years that the silence of no desire has remained in me," the Shaikh answered. "I have become clear as an unscratched mirror. When the thought of roasted sheep's head entered my mind and whetted my appetite and became a desire, I knew that that belonged to our friend yonder. For the mirror of silence is without any image of itself; if an image shows in the mirror, it is the image of another."

Intuition Application: Open to Nothing

Take some predetermined time to do nothing except close your eyes and ears. Daydream, take an imaginary shower of different-colored light, go to your imagined favorite place, or simply have no agenda. The most important thing is to do it for at least the full time you promised yourself.

Stimulation

Boredom kills. So much of our work becomes the same old thing, time and time again. We get worn down and ultimately become inefficient by the repetition. Repetition is for machines. We need to be recharged; intuition does this by breaking up routine and allowing unplanned spontaneity. It is the perfect medium for our "economy of surprise," such as out-of-the-blue e-mails, job opportunities, and unforeseen problems that come up and need to be taken care of in the moment. Surprise is energy and resource! Jump on it, use it.

Let Go

We stress ourselves out because we have been taught to maintain control, to keep things in order, to make sure and double sure that we do the right things in the right way. But these days, things are out of control— and who knows the right answer anyway? It's time to let go. Break away from the belief that you must have a grip on everything. Surrender to the force, the life force that is inherently in control and that surfaces through intuition. It takes a kind of spiritual perspective of acceptance and even reverence for the originating life source to follow the intuitive voice. If we just heed the call, we find our way. All good things flow from that.

The River of Life

> "The world is ruled by letting things take their water course. It cannot be ruled by interfering."
> —Lao Tsu, *Tao Te Ching*

An effective way of picturing intuitive working and living is through the idea of a river. Intuitions are an endless river of impulses. There is a constant streaming in our lives on this water planet, and by consciously going with the flow, we are not resisting, fighting, defending—all of which takes great, great energy, and which is self-defeating and life denying. Keep flowing with the inner river of feeling and you will be supported, although at times there are bumps, rocks, curves, and falls. As water, keep flowing and you will be taken through the lows.

Intuition Application: Become Watery

Intuitives are like water —
open, nonresistant,
adaptable, reflective, soft,
nurturing, refreshing, cleansing,
moving,
energizing

Which of these watery qualities speaks to you the most now? In becoming that quality, what does your intuition say to do now?

Learning

> "If we don't change, we don't grow. If we don't grow, we are not really living. Growth demands a temporary surrender of security."
>
> —Gail Sheehy

Renewing, regenerating, reinventing are all a function of learning and growing. Intuition is naturally a growing force, constantly absorbing and digesting new information and experience. If we allow it to speak to us, it mentors with great accumulated wisdom that keeps accumulating.

Joseph Galerneau, head of executive training at AT&T, allots about one-fifth of his $3.5 million budget to courses that encourage "introspection." He explains, "This company is not going to be successful unless we have people who can learn from experience. We need our people to be accountable and responsible for managing their own piece of the business. It takes a certain amount of reflection to do this successfully." [20]

Intuition Application: Become a Learner

What does your intuition tell you that you need to learn? What is the first beginning step to learn that?

Break It Up!

> "Every act of creation is first of all an act of destruction."
>
> —Pablo Picasso

When we become fixed on a fixed way with a fixed pattern, we block new learning. Without growing, we die inside, and we do not survive either in life or in business. Really, the best way to fix our lives is to break it up, to open the dam of suppressed energy, passion, and creativity.

> "Sacred cows make great steaks."
> —Richard Nicolosi

Intuition Application: The Breakout Feeling

What feels fixed, stuck, dense, and immobile in your life? How would it feel to break it up and break out? Describe the physical sensation. A good way to start the break-up process is to shake out the body to loosen it up.

Joy

> "Work is love made visible."
> —Kahlil Gibran, *The Prophet*

So much of our burnout is the result of not doing what we enjoy. If your heart isn't into it, you will be out of it. There is no way we can keep going and sustain high performance and excellence levels unless we love what we do. If we follow our intuition, we do what makes us feel good. Intuitive working is flowing with what I call the "feel good factor." If you are true to it, however, it may mean changing your occupation, your partner-ships, your lifestyle. For sure, it means having more fun at work. Great things get done with the spirit of play. It is in play that the magical, intuitive child comes out in each of us. Our natural genius shines forth through a joyous attitude.

So much of our occupational dis-ease is the result of not doing what is fulfilling. We take a job because it seems practical, pays well, or is what we have been told would be good for us to do. Intuitive working is happy work because it's the work that feels good to us.

Intuition is the transmission of our true joy. When work is deeply satisfying and meaningful, nothing need be forced and fitted.

According to psychologist, Mihaly Csikszentmihaly, in his research documented in *Flow: The Psychology of Optimal Experience,* "When we are in this state of working with joy, we lose sense of time and self, and are at our peak efficiency, creativity, and state of 'aliveness.'"

The intuitive way is a different work ethic. Instead of work as hard, and discipline as good, work becomes joyous and easy, and discipline becomes ultimately unproductive if we are continually forcing ourselves to do what we don't want to be doing.

Intuition Application: The Feel-Good Work Treat

Try this "feel-good" way of working by taking a set amount of time during your day to do only what feels good. Try it, you'll like it—and you'll get things done!

Simplicity: Way of the Fool

> "Let him become a fool that he may become wise."
> —from I Corinthians iii, 18–19

Others, including your own inner judge and critic, will consider you a fool, a simpleton, for following such a simplistic way of feeling your way through life. It's true what Einstein said, "Life is a process of groping." Life has become so complex that there may be no other way. Remember, it was a simple child who saw that the emperor had no clothes.

> "It is only the fool who becomes anything."
> —Fyodor Dostoyevsky

126   When you are on to your intuitive truth, you will jump the fences of conventional wisdom. You will be called crazy or deluded. Good! Then you know you are on the right path. Bless them and keep going. Intuition does not stop at tradition. Everyone who has made their fortune and created their destiny went beyond the accepted norm. They all flew in the face of the prevailing winds. Remember, it takes a wind in your face to get your plane off the runway. It's time to fly.

> "Those who danced were thought to be quite insane by those who could not hear the music."
> —Angela Monet

I suppose somebody would have initially called Conrad Hilton crazy for following his intuition in the following situation. He relates in his autobiography that, "My first bid for my first hotel building was $165,000. Then somehow that didn't feel right to me. Another figure kept coming, $180,000. It satisfied me. It felt right! I changed my bid to the larger figure on that hunch. When the bids were opened, the closest bid to mine was $179,800. I won by $200. Eventually the assets returned me $2 million." [21]

Intuition Application: Take the Dare

What is something you consider crazy or foolish but would love to do? I dare you to try it!

> "It was a day like this that Marco Polo set out for
> China. What are *your* plans for today?"
>
> —Anonymous

Red Flags

> "Stress makes people stupid."
>
> —Anonymous manager

Intuitive judgment is impeded and skewed when we are off our center. This happens through fatigue, stress, burnout, fear, greed, depression, anger, illness—extreme states of being. Intuition thrives on balance. Again, the more you know yourself, the better you realize when you are out of your balance. Actually, your intuition will signal you to regain your equilibrium. Intuition will instruct you how to rebalance. Remember, intuition is our healer—our inborn doctor, psychologist, and counselor.

12 THE INTUITIVE FUTURE LIFE

A New Way of Being

> "The most exciting breakthrough of the 21ˢᵗ century will occur not because of technology, but because of an expanding concept of what it means to be human."
> —John Naisbitt, *Megatrends 2000*

Looking intuitively into the future through my feeling eye, I will use the various intuition applications described in this book. Starting with the *bracketing* process, what do my various emotional states—paranoid fear, passionate desire, and peaceful balance— suggest?

The Paranoid Future

As I feel into my stomach and its remembrances of *fear*, I see things spinning out of control into violent chaos. What comes to my mind's eye is a vision of billions of individuals totally dependent upon robotic machine systems that self-replicate their own breakdowns and viruses, with DNA cloning gone awry and everyone having in their own hands the nanotechnology to easily destroy the world. The human heart of love and compassion has been destroyed by the addiction to technology and artifice. Our humanity is dead, and the species wiped out, done in by our own "intelligence." Chilling, white plague. Possible? Yes.

But once we have previewed, we can prevent and preempt. How? By taking to heart the richness and beauty of the human soul of emotion. To preserve our humanity and to save our species from extinction, we must revere that which makes us human—our feelings. And that is why intuition is so imperative.

The Passionate Future

On the other side, my *passionate projection* for what I would love to see about the future is literally felt in my heart and suggests the picture of all our technological, economic, and social advances bringing us to a new state of sustainable, peaceful, healthy, abundant, creative, and meaningful life—all of which makes us happy! Unless we are happy, what good is all the rest? And it is impossible to be truly happy unless we are authentic—true to our feelings. There is simply no way we can be happy with ourselves and others unless we can express how we are feeling, whatever we are feeling. The intuitive future life of happiness demands attention to our feelings, accepts them, values them, and acts on them.

The Peaceful Future

My inner state of *balanced peace* is felt in my solar plexus, halfway between the horrors of an upset stomach and the ecstatic high of a light heart. This feeling of peace suggests that the probable future is a survivable muddle—that we will grope along, somehow staving off dehumanization, while achieving an enhanced quality of life, though it will be beset by great inequalities.

The Intuitive Future

Futures are made, and in the intuitive world they are made by individuals following their deepest intention and purpose. When I ask my intuition what I genuinely want of life, it reveals the *intention* to seek the best possible, to live the dream, to go for what I would love to see—the intuitive life.

Intuition is an opening to the wonders that lie within us. By tapping our true selves through our honest feelings, we access our natural genius, the genius of being ourselves. Who knows what can come of that? Perhaps a whole new way of living that produces new ways of relating and of doing business and politics. Perhaps a whole new type of innovation, creativity, and intelligence that is heartfelt. Perhaps a whole new value system, a deeper humanization, an evolved human that is not marked so much by external tools and goodies but by a richness of consciousness, love, and expression— where we measure ourselves by the depth and authenticity of our personal being.

In this intuitive state of living, we make better decisions for ourselves with greater purpose and intention, and we act on those decisions without hesitation. Yet we are fully adaptable to change as we create and re-create ourselves, all the while partnering and relating with honesty and happiness and with a tremendous zest and renewable energy that powers the body. We won't need so much, work so hard, or get run down to the point of having to constantly acquire new limbs and pills to prop us up.

How do we get there? How do we *create* this? Start now by feeling what you are feeling, and be true to those feelings. Become more, more of yourself. *Act* on this with belief, balance, and courage. From intuition, move into what I call "intuaction." *Intuact!* Perhaps our finest legacy as a species is that we found a way to survive and thrive on.

It's time to wake up! It's time to break free of our collective hypnosis of following the herd and of going along with the old, obsolete stories of life. We have the window of opportunity now to break set, to make up a new map of life that does not come from "thinking" one up or from modeling others' behavior but from the highest expression of the universe as we know it—ourselves—the feeling, breathing, moving, intentional, whole person.

> "What is the most fascinating thing on Earth? My own Being. I, a microcosm of the Universe."
> —Robert Muller

The Future Is Our Friend

So often we fear the future. We do not trust it. We seem to expect the worst. It is clear to me, however, that if we discover and act with conviction on our core purpose for being, the future will take care of itself. Like a seed that has a genetic code and unfolds and blossoms accordingly, the seed of our future being is planted in the dark insides of our inner, inner self. We sow the seed by acting on our innermost feeling. We reap the seed by the everyday adjustments, revealed by our intuitions, that service our originating core purpose.

Intuition Application: The Preferred Vision

Close your eyes and picture how you would like to be ten to twenty years from now. Don't hold back your dreams. Go for it. Don't be shy, don't be modest. No wimps allowed. Be bold, be aggressive, be brave. See your desired future in light, color, and detail.

> "Help us to be ever faithful gardeners of the spirit, who know that without darkness nothing comes to birth, and without light nothing flowers."
> —May Sarton

NOTES

1. "Gut Feelings Tracked to the Source: The Brain," *New York Times,* March 4, 1997.

2. Karen O. Dowd and Jeanne Liedtka, "What Corporations Seek in MBA Hires: A Survey," *The Magazine of the Graduate Management Council,* Winter 1994.

3. Weston Agor, *Intuition in Organizations* (Thousand Oaks, CA: Sage Publications, Inc., 1989).

4. Tony Buzan and Barry Buzan, *The Mind Map Book* (New York: Penguin Putnam, Plume, 1996).

5. Scott Kirsner, "The Ultimate Guide to Internet Deals," *Fast Company,* no. 24 (May 1999).

6. Marcia Emery, *Dr. Marcia Emery's Intuition Workbook* (New Jersey: Prentice-Hall, 1994).

7. Nancy Rosanoff, *Intuition Workout* (Fairfield, CT: Aslan Publishing, 1991).

8. "Survival of the Quickest," *San Jose Mercury News,* May 17, 1995.

9. Bruce Pandolfini, "All the Right Moves," *Fast Company,* no. 24 (May 1999).

10. *Harvard Business Review,* in *Intuition Magazine,* Vol. 2, No. 1.

11. *International Journal of Science Education,* quoted in *Intuition Magazine,* Vol. 2, No.1.

12. *Wall Street Journal,* in *Intuition Magazine,* Vol. 2, No. 1.

13. Sharon Begley and Joshua Cooper Ramo, "The Puzzle of Genius," *Newsweek* (June 28, 1993).

14. Natasha Raymond, "Human Lie Detector," *Psychology Today* (September 2000).

15. Ibid.

16. Stephanie Osfield, *New Woman* (March 1997).

17. Daniel Goleman, *Working with Emotional Intelligence* (New York: Bantam Books, 1998).

18. "Characteristics of Top Salespeople," *Selling Power,* (September 1998).

19. Daniel Pink, "Metaphor Marketing," *Fast Company* (April/May 1998).

20. Stratford Sherman, "Leaders Learn to Heed the Voice Within," *Fortune* (August 22, 1994).

21. Barbara Schultz, *Intuition Magazine,* Vol. 2 No.1.